What All Customers Want

(And Everyone Is a Customer)

A "How To" Guide for
Superior Customer Service
in the 21st Century

David Driskill

Dale,
One time client, trusted
Financial Advisor and good
Friend, I can't thank you
enough For your counsel
over the years.
I hope you Find the book
interesting

David
July 2023

Published by: HRD Press, Inc.
                    22 Amherst Road
                    Amherst, MA 01002
                    800-822-2801 (U.S. and Canada)
                    413-253-3488
                    413-253-3490 (fax)
                    http://www.hrdpress.com

ISBN 978-1-61014-475-9

For Marianne

Table of Contents

*"Customer service should not be a department.
It should be the entire company."*

—Tony Hsieh & Taylor Chastain

*"A customer is the most important visitor on our premises;
he is not dependent on us. We are dependent on him. He is
not an interruption in our work. He is the purpose of it. He
is not an outsider in our business. He is part of it. We are
not doing him a favor by serving him. He is doing us a favor
by giving us an opportunity to do so."*

—Mahatma Gandhi

Introduction

*A customer is anyone in a position to feel satisfied or dissatisfied about what "you" *do **and** a customer is able to act on their satisfaction or dissatisfaction.*

This book is about customer** service. More specifically, this book provides

1. an inclusive definition of the customer (above),
2. a description of the fundamental ingredients of every customer service organization, and
3. a thorough description and specific examples of the interconnected components of what every customer wants from their service provider.

The components of what customers want from their service provider are *constants that are relevant across industries, eras, and technology cycles.*

Failing to deliver all of what the customer wants increases the likelihood of customer dissatisfaction and, in the extreme, can become a catalyst for that customer becoming a powerful and negative voice in the marketplace. In complete contrast, delivering the components of what all customers want increases the likelihood of customer satisfaction and, under certain circumstances, even loyalty—creating an advocate for the service provider. In short, *there's a lot at stake for everyone.*

This book has four main attributes:

1. **It's straightforward:** The language used, concepts presented, and recommendations made are all accessible to the reader (e.g., limited jargon, well-defined and limited use of acronyms).

---

* The word "you" is both literal and representational. It is literal as it applies to every individual involved in or even peripherally experiences service delivery. It is representational as it applies to organizations or teams in the service delivery process.

** The word "customer" used throughout this book instead of the word "client." This is a choice. Client is often a reference to a *customer* using professional services. Since customer is the root, it is used throughout this book.

2. **It's practical:** Readers can readily apply the principles, specific concepts, and recommendations presented, all supported by a diverse set of specific application examples.

3. **It's innovative:** It combines and interrelates concepts and ideas that, when applied, produce original, productive, and even surprising results (e.g., service problems can lead to customer loyalty if the problem is handled in a certain way).

4. **It's Ambitious:** This book provides a practical, applicable answer to some big questions, not least, "How do we ensure customer satisfaction with the delivery of services?"

For whom was this book written?

It's tempting to say that this book is for everyone who receives or delivers service. It's tempting because almost everyone has a stake in customer service. However, realistically, this book is *not* for everyone. This book is targeted at service providers. More specifically, this book is for:

- Executive (C-Suite) management and senior operations management of customer service organizations—whether they serve individual customers or other businesses.

- Supervisory and front-line management personnel charged with developing, directing, and monitoring service delivery to customers.

- Individual customer service employees interested in increasing their knowledge and in honing their customer service skills.

- Training professionals charged with the development of customer service personnel at all levels (e.g., skills training, management development, new employee orientation).

- Human resource professionals charged with developing and reinforcing the corporate culture and values of the service provider organization.

- Students, teachers, and other academics interested in learning about customer service and the practical application of that learning.

- Others with a vested interest in customer service (e.g., service provider board members, process improvement or reengineering professionals, customer service consultants).

Why is this book important?

First: The short answer to the question above is, *"because we can do better."* And because there's more at stake today than yesterday, and there will be more at stake tomorrow. Why? Because, to repeat the often-used phrase, "the voice of the customer"—it has become louder and louder. Social media has enabled a single customer to talk to hundreds, thousands, even millions of others. Because service providers have asked customers for their input, the customer has given it and will continue to do so at unprecedented levels. In turn, to the extent that it is in the public domain, the results of all of this customer input influences existing and potential customers. From this book, you will learn how to deliver customer satisfaction, even delight, and in so doing, ensure that the voice of your customer reflects your understanding of who your customers are, what they want, and your commitment to deliver superior service.

Second: In addition to empowered customers, employees have an increasingly influential voice. And as you will find later, employees have all the attributes of a customer—*they are customers.* As such, employees can now speak out more than ever before. Yes, there are still some companies that try to suppress the voice of their employees, especially when that voice is critical or problematic (e.g., recommending process changes the provider is unwilling to make). But more and more, employees can say what they want, when they want, to whom they want. Certainly, this new, louder voice has been misused and has unfairly targeted both individuals and organizations. But it has also been a voice for positive change regarding the work environment, calling out process and product flaws, gender, and racial bias as well as the historic patriarchy. From this book, you will learn the specific steps you need to implement and behaviors you need to exhibit to treat your managers, colleagues, and employees as true customers—*because they are.*

Third: This book is important because delivering satisfying service to customers (of all kinds) *is the right thing to do.* Putting a moral twist on service delivery in what is essentially a business book may seem like an oxymoron. And for some, the claim "it is the right thing to do" will fall on deaf ears. For others, those for whom doing the right thing is an important value, it makes sense. Service providers have a moral obligation to deliver service effectively to their customers.

Many customers come to the service encounter expecting, or at least hoping, that they will be treated with respect, interact with someone who listens, and be told the truth, among other service behaviors. By contrast, some customers come to the service encounter cynically, or even with a sense of dread because of how they've been treated in the past. It's up to the effective service provider to surprise this second group of customers with an entirely positive service experience.

There has been some recent research about whether or not doing good is good for business—with mixed results. Most of this research is concerned with businesses engaged in socially responsible behavior (e.g., environmental action, socially responsible investing). When it comes to treating customers and employees as customers effectively, it seems self-evident that doing so is good for business. There is also research to support this assertion.*

I will further assert that doing the right thing for customers and everyone around you, treating everyone like a valued customer is good for everyone, including you. *You'll sleep better.*

Four Important Factors this Book
Does Not Address

1. **Price:** While obviously important, individual employees providing customer service and service provider organizations are typically not setting the parameters for pricing. This book is about the factors the service provider *can* control.

2. **Product Quality:** Similar to pricing, product quality influences customer satisfaction. But again, the service provider is not in control of this important variable *unless the service is the product,* which will be addressed extensively throughout this book.

3. **Brand Loyalty:** Some customers are loyal to specific brands. This loyalty is a kind of emotional wild-card that can eclipse cost, product features, and service quality in importance (e.g., Apple vs. PC or Android and vice versa).

---

* Adams, R.L., "10 Reasons Why Good Customer Service is Your Most Important Metric," Entrepreneur (On-Line magazine), December 12, 2016

4. **Subjective Moral/Political Decision Making:** A customer decision and action because of a perceived lapse or emphasis on moral behavior or a political position (e.g., boycotting a company employing child labor in Asia, or only engaging in socially responsible investing). For these customers, *price, product, and service quality are not a primary consideration.*

A Little History

As a self-employed management consultant, I've been a service provider for over 40 years. I worked in corrections (prisons), law enforcement, for the Defense Department (as a sub-contractor), in healthcare, and financial services, among other industries. I did project work, delivered training, and sometimes acted as a mediator between service providers and their customers. I also developed and managed hundreds of customer surveys, always using expert assistance when needed. It is from all the work I did and the experiences I have had that this book finds its source, especially the customer surveys.

For a long time, since at least into the early 2000s, I claimed the ingredients of this book as my sole creation. In the other work I did, I always tried to be scrupulous about citing my sources. But when it came to defining the customer and what all customers want, I felt ownership. I felt that I had devised a new and innovative way to define customers and the basic interconnected components of what they wanted.

I was wrong. I discovered everything that follows in this book from surveying and talking with customers to working with service providers. Customers and service providers told me everything that follows. They didn't use the same terminology. They certainly didn't organize the content the way I have, or articulated the interdependencies of what customers want, but they did disclose their values, wants, and needs as both customers and service providers.

Thus, *What All Customers Want* represents the true *voice of the customer*—the voice of *your* customer. In this book, their voices come through from literally thousands of surveys and conversations with customers of all kinds, from the classic external customer calling for service, and senior executives of organizations receiving service from other organizations (B2B), to internal employees who, as

[5]

will be detailed later, have all the attributes of a customer. As you will see, all these customers want the same things. All these customers want to *matter* to their service provider. All these customers want their service provider to do the right thing, even when the customer may not know exactly what the right thing is.

As was stated earlier, this book is not for everyone. This book is not for individuals or organizations that aren't interested in the voice of their customers. This comment may sound disingenuous; after all, doesn't everyone want to hear the voice of their customer? *No, they don't.* Some providers think they know best. Some providers look down on their customers. These comments don't come from a research report or an article in a business magazine, they come from my direct observations. I've been in organizations or departments where the customer is viewed as a necessary evil, an irritant. I've met individual providers who see customers as only a means to an end, not worthy of respectful or professional service. I'd like to think that anyone reading this book would be influenced for the better, but I'm all grown up and magical thinking is not in my repertoire.

The above being said, I'm not cynical. In my direct experience, there are far more service provider organizations and individuals who *do* want to hear and respond effectively to the voice of the customer than those who don't. There are far more service organizations and individuals who respect their customers than those who don't. There are far more service organizations and individuals who want to do the "right thing," than those who don't. This book is most assuredly for these organizations and individuals. In this book, they will find practical ideas, tools, and examples of how to deliver truly superior customer service.

A Warning and a Request

Over my career, I've developed a number of tools to manage and improve service quality. For example, many years ago I developed a behavioral checklist with an associated guidebook to monitor and provide feedback to telephone customer service representatives (CSRs). I developed the content of the checklist and supporting materials based on my academic background in psychology, monitoring hundreds of service calls, and systematically gathering input from working CSRs. The checklist I developed was probably not the first of its kind, but it was certainly one of the first.

However, over the years, and in some instances, the checklist has calcified into a rigid and arbitrary tool; a tool that when employed arbitrarily, might fail to capture the nuances of a particular call or the needs of a particular customer. Worst yet, sticking rigidly to these protocols might punish an employee for doing something outside the checklist, but who responded effectively to the customer. Likewise, it might reward an employee for staying with the checklist instead of responding skillfully and flexibly to the customer.

So, here's the warning and the request. Don't let anything presented in this book, or any book, theory, or tool, become fixed and immutable. Don't assume that something that makes sense today will always make sense. Don't ever become so attached to any particular theory or approach that anything that contradicts it feels like heresy.

I think that what follows in this book makes sense; the concepts presented can be used to better understand customer service, both historically and prospectively. One of my main goals in writing this book is to get people—you—thinking. I would be happy to find out that what follows is incomplete, or that there is a better, clearer way to explain, understand, and apply what is presented here. *That's progress.*

Right or wrong, the customer is always right.
—Marshall Field

In any great organization, it is far, far safer to be wrong with the majority than to be right alone.
—John Kenneth Galbraith

Chapter 1

Defining the Customer and the Ingredients of a Customer Service Organization

This chapter provides a detailed and inclusive definition of the customer. It goes on to describe and provide prescriptive examples of the fundamental elements of the customer service organization. This sets the stage for subsequent chapters which provide a comprehensive description of what all customers want (WACW) from their service provider.

The motivation for developing both the content and sequence that follows is to enable readers to examine their organization, their various customers, and their performance in serving those customers. From such an examination and using the ideas and tools from all the information, ideas, and recommendations that follow, service providers can do the work to ensure a satisfying, sometimes even delightful, experience for customers.

1. Defining the Customer

If customer satisfaction and all that it entails is the common and strategic goal of all service providers, then a definition of "customer" and the exact nature of what constitutes a "customer" must be defined. In fact, the definition is integral to the practical application of all of the information, ideas, and recommendations presented and discussed in this book. Thus, the following definition is presented as a kind of touchstone for *all* that follows:

> *A customer is anyone in a position to feel satisfied or dissatisfied about what "you" do, and a customer is able to act on their satisfaction or dissatisfaction.*

To some, defining the customer may seem unnecessary and simplistic. We all have a sense of what a customer is—someone buying goods or services. For some, their definition of a customer is broad enough to include both internal and external personnel because their experience indicates that internal personnel share many of the same attributes and desires as the traditionally defined external customer.

I've asked this question to thousands of employees and managers: What is a customer? What defines a customer? After thinking about the question, their responses often included *both* external and internal customers. However, their definition of an internal customer was narrow. Most often, it is focused on the relationship between support areas within an organization and their service to "front-line" (external) customer service staff. On occasion, responses to my question included the opinion that a person's boss was somehow a customer that must be satisfied. Also on occasion, a respondent would answer by saying that everyone is a customer. While this is the correct response, it was often a kind of "throw away" comment—a politically correct aphorism without an underlying understanding about the implications of such a definition.

A completely inclusive definition of a customer is *anyone in a position to feel satisfied or dissatisfied about what you do; and a customer is able to act on their satisfaction or dissatisfaction*. Such a definition includes *everyone* directly or peripherally in the service chain—from the classic external customer to the person sitting in the next cubicle, to your boss and to building maintenance personnel. This totally inclusive definition carries the risk of sounding right, but not having the underlying supportive substance. It is so broad and inclusive that, unless it is supported by specific examples, it can be as practically useless as the statement, "all babies should eat good food." We can all agree, but so what?

The "so what" is a practical understanding of the universal interdependency of everyone in the service chain: a practical and even empathic understanding about the nature of everyone's responsibilities to everyone else and the consequences of success and failure of meeting those responsibilities. Understanding this can be used as the basis for action in the form of behavior, task performance, or technical support, that satisfies or potentially delights the customers that surround everyone. (Note that the word "potential" is used. The only leap of faith here is to assert that there is a greater likelihood of satisfying a customer if we define them as a customer to begin with.)

The first part of the inclusive definition says that everyone is a customer. Again, this isn't only a politically correct or "throw away" comment. It is the literal truth. Everyone in the service organization coming into direct or indirect contact with any other individual or group in the service delivery process can perceive behavior, task

[10]

performance, and outcomes. Immediately subsequent, or even coincident, with that perception, a reaction will occur. The reaction will typically be positive or negative. People don't tend to feel neutral. The perceiver will feel good or bad, satisfied or dissatisfied, about their experience—often while the experience is unfolding.

The idea that people react and qualitatively judge all their experiences is supportable anecdotally and empirically. A thought experiment illustrates the support for the immediacy of qualitative judgment. Simply think about meeting someone for the first time. Ask yourself: how long did it take to decide whether you liked or disliked the person (even slightly)? When asked this question, most people will admit—some reluctantly—that they judged the new acquaintance in seconds. Most people are quick to point out that they are also able to modify this "first impression" as time goes by, but their first reaction remains, and may remain influential.

Empirical evidence also supports the suggestion that our qualitative judgment of experience is immediate and often profound. The study of the biological basis of behavior indicates that we are "hardwired" to judge situations and experiences automatically, emotionally, and very quickly.* In fact, our evolution as a species depended—and depends—on our ability to quickly and accurately observe or otherwise experience our surroundings and the people in them and then quickly formulate a judgement. The classic example illustrating this point is often referred to as the "fight or flight" response. Both fight and flight are emotional responses. Stated somewhat simplistically, the emotions enable rapid actions because of increased adrenalin. We have evolved to fight when cornered, run away from threats, and even though it is not included in the typical discussion, approach an attractive or survival enhancing event, person, or object.

Ironically, people often react negatively to the notion that we are "hardwired" to behave in a certain manner. After all, we do not perceive ourselves as automatons, bereft of free will and simply playing some biologically prescribed script. To satisfy these objections, it can quickly be acknowledged that our biologically driven reactions can

---

* "Thinking, Fast and Slow," Kahneman, Daniel, Farrar, Straus and Giroux, (2011) and "Emotions and Types of Emotional Responses," Cherry, Kendra, verywellmind, (2022).

and are modified by our rational selves. We can think "slow." We can choose not to be a slave to our first reaction. We can train ourselves to be deliberative and analytical. We can, in fact, learn to not "judge a book by its cover" over the long-term. However, we cannot deny our fundamental nature. We do judge the "cover," and that initial reaction can have an outsized role in our overall reaction to a person or a situation.

Another objection to the notion of our predilection to be satisfied or dissatisfied with all or any part of our experience is the argument by some people that they are neutral. These people suggest that they approach experience "unconditionally," and that they only form a judgment after rational analysis. Rather than argue with this point of view, it can simply be acknowledged that some people go through the cycle of immediate and emotional reaction to rational analysis more quickly than others.

The application of the forgoing discussion is that if you experience all or any part of the service request or delivery process, or almost any other experience at home or work, most of us will automatically judge that experience. Further, virtually all customers *can* act based on their initial and ongoing satisfaction or dissatisfaction. The customer may choose not to act, to act minimally, or act decisively with significant impact.

> So, specifically, who judges the service experience—who is the customer?

The External Customer

The external customer can feel satisfied or dissatisfied about the service delivery and can act based on that satisfaction or dissatisfaction. The service experience by the external customers may be entirely positive, entirely negative, or have both positive and negative elements. If the experience is entirely positive, it can be inferred that the customer is satisfied and their subsequent action, if any, might include expressing satisfaction (if asked), additional or expanded use of the provider, recommending the provider to others, and entering the next service interaction with a positive expectation. If the experience is entirely negative, it can be inferred that their subsequent action, if any, might include a direct complaint to the service provider, telling others about their negative experience, choosing another service provider in the future, or entering the next service encounter with negative expectations. In the case of a mix of satisfaction and dissatisfaction, the customer may be willing and able to discriminate the "good" from the "bad." For example, after being politely told that what the customer wants cannot be provided, the customer may be dissatisfied with not getting what they want, but some customers (regrettably very few) may acknowledge the polite behavior of the service representative. Other customers will be unable or unwilling to discriminate the "good" from the "bad" and define the entire experience as bad, and then act based on that judgement.

> **A Note about Customer Needs vs. Wants:** In customer service, needs tend to be concrete requirements anchored to specific, baseline requirements. For example, customers need accurate information, data, or guidance from their provider. Failing to meet this need not only dissatisfies the customer, but it may also put the customer in a vulnerable, imperiled position (e.g., they make flawed, even costly decisions based on inaccurate provider input). A customer's want is less basic than a need and more subjective. For example, the customer may want concierge level, customized service from a provider ill-equipped to provide it (e.g., a large volume contact center not structured to provide personalized service). If what the customer wants (no matter how unreasonable) isn't provided, they may be dissatisfied.
>
> One way to offset this dissatisfaction is educating customers about reasonable and limited expectations for service delivery. For customers who perceive themselves as VIPs, setting limited expectations may not work, but for most, it may prevent extreme dissatisfaction from not having "wants" addressed.

According to the White House Office of Consumer Affairs, dissatisfied customers tell 9 to 15 people or more about their negative experience. According to Salesforce, satisfied customers will tell 6 or more people. However, these projections fall apart if the customer is also an active internet user or even an internet influencer—with thousands, sometimes hundreds of thousands of followers.

A second factor to consider are customer reviews. It has become commonplace to survey customers after their service experience. It is also common for prospective customers to read some reviews prior to engaging with a provider. The potential voice of the customer is loud and pervasive and their ability to act, using the internet as a kind of megaphone, has never been greater. This pervasive sharing on the internet shows no signs of abating.

The Service Representative's Supervisor and Manager are Customers

Clearly, the service representative's front-line supervisor and manager are both in a position to feel satisfied or dissatisfied about their employees. If they are satisfied, they can advance the employee, provide added compensation (or bonuses), provide expanded resources (e.g., training, rotational assignments), etc. By contrast, if the supervisor and manager are dissatisfied with their employee, they can withhold opportunities and, among other actions, employ disciplinary measures up to and including termination.

In addition to the highly tangible actions a supervisor or manager may take, the satisfied or dissatisfied supervisor or manager may act to foster a certain kind of environment depending on how they feel about an individual employee or even an entire team. The satisfied supervisor might foster a friendly, highly cooperative environment; the dissatisfied supervisor might foster an environment of distrust or isolation. It's a mistake to think that only the tangible, material actions matter. Less tangible, more subjective actions can have an equivalent or even greater impact. For example, a supervisor may feel dissatisfied with a specific employee, with or without cause, and, as a result, communicate their dissatisfaction nonverbally (e.g., not making eye contact, frowning whenever the employee offers input during a meeting). By contrast, a supervisor might communicate their satisfaction with other employees with a positive facial expression and engaging in social/personal communication (e.g., "What did you do this weekend?). Unfortunately, supervisor bias for or against employees may be fixed (e.g., a function of their core personality) and be unaffected by employee behavior. However, as customers, most supervisors will be influenced by employee behavior and performance.

Support Personnel are Customers

Often the front-line service representative relies on support personnel to provide service to the external customer. Support personnel might include IT people or what is often referred to as "back-office" personnel supplying research assistance, work/data processing, background data, or information. Support personnel can feel satisfied or dissatisfied with the front-line service representative. If the service representative is patient, polite, professional, and acknowledges the help of support personnel, support staff are likely to feel satisfied. As a result, the support personnel are more likely to *want* to help the front-line service representative and may go out of their way to do so. By contrast, if the service representative expresses impatience, abrupt and demanding behavior or other behavior that offends support personnel, support staff are likely to feel dissatisfied. They will still provide support but may do so by meeting only minimal requirements; they might be unmotivated and, at the extreme, support personnel may sabotage a service representative they don't like by providing incomplete, false, or even deliberately misleading information.

Front-Line Employees are Customers of their Supervisors and Managers

Employees of all types and at all levels will feel satisfied or dissatisfied with their immediate supervisor and manager. There are a myriad of drivers of employee satisfaction and dissatisfaction with their bosses. An authoritarian, bullying boss, or a boss who fails to provide sufficient support to their employees, is likely to engender dissatisfied employees. By contrast, a boss who treats employees with respect, provides timely and useful feedback, and delivers on promises of support, advancement, and guidance, is likely to have satisfied employees. Satisfied employees are likely to be motivated, productive, and emulate the positive behavior of their boss. Dissatisfied employees are likely to be less motivated, less productive, and their dissatisfaction may end up being expressed by quitting.

People leave their jobs for a host of reasons. A recent survey by Forbes identified the top five reasons for employees to want to quit:[*]

1. Toxic company culture
2. Low salary
3. Poor management
4. Lack of healthy work/life boundaries
5. Not allowing for remote work

---

[*] "Discover the Top Five Reasons Workers Want to Quit Their Jobs," Robinson, Bryan, *Forbes* (online) May 2022

> It's worth noting that employees have been gaining power during recent years (especially during the pandemic). We've seen "the great resignation." We've also seen inappropriate customer behavior be called into account. If an airline passenger behaves in an aggressive, threatening manner, they will likely be met at the gate by law enforcement, face fines, and even jail time. While gender and racial bias continues, such behavior is less and less acceptable and often produces very negative consequences. All these examples indicate a change in the power dynamic between employees, employers and their customers.

Notice that Toxic Culture and Poor Management are on the list above, both of which can be a function of either or both corporate culture and individual manager/supervisor behavior.

Going back to 2017, a Gallup poll of over 1 million employees concluded that the number one reason people quit their jobs, "is a bad boss or immediate supervisor."[**]

It should be acknowledged once again that the action resulting from satisfaction or dissatisfaction can be highly tangible (quitting) or more subjective (a good attitude). It should also be noted that dissatisfied employees may not demonstrate any overt action. For example, even when a job becomes joyless for an employee, they stay in the position because they need the job. This is not a desirable state for anyone in the service chain.

In their role of service provider to their employees as customers, supervisors and managers would do well to remember a quote from Goethe: *"The way you see people is the way you treat them, and the way you treat them is what they become."*

Colleagues are Customers

In the classic work setting, and even the work-at-home setting, all the employees in each team are one another's customers. They can feel satisfied or dissatisfied with their colleagues individually or as a group and they can act based on their satisfaction or dissatisfaction. If satisfied, members of the team support one another willingly and

---

[**] "The No.1 Employee Benefit That No One's Talking About," Nolan, Tom, Gallup (online)

are likely to "pitch in" if one or more members of their team are overloaded with work or under a tight deadline. If dissatisfied with the team or a specific team member, they are less likely to volunteer their help and if asked or told to help, they may be unmotivated or reluctantly provide support.

The Service Provider is a Customer of the External Customer

While it may be counter intuitive, remaining faithful to the definition of what attributes constitute a customer, the service provider can feel satisfied or dissatisfied with the external customer and act as a result. If the customer supplies correct information, is polite, patient, and generally behaves in a respectful way, the service representative is likely to feel satisfied with the external customer and, in turn, provide responsive, timely, and accurate service. By contrast, if the external customer is rude, demanding, and disrespectful, the service representative will probably still do their job, but they may do so reluctantly, at a minimally acceptable level, and be unlikely to make any extra effort on behalf of the external customer.

Institutions as Customers to Other Institutions (Business-to-Business or B2B)

Companies from many lines of business can be in a customer, service provider relationship. For example, large investment management companies (e.g., Charles Schwab, Fidelity, T. Rowe Price) are B2B customers of large custodial banks (e.g., BNW Mellon, Northern Trust, State Street Bank). The investment companies rely on the custodial banks for a myriad of services, from processing millions of transactions totaling trillions of dollars, to computing and reporting the stock prices to the media. Other examples of B2B customers abound; insurance underwriters serving insurance brokers, database management firms serving the data access needs of other institutions (e.g., libraries, hospitals), independent travel agencies supporting the travel needs of corporate clients, etc.

The B2B customer can be satisfied or dissatisfied with their institutional service provider and can act based on their satisfaction or dissatisfaction. However, a crucial difference between an individual customer and the B2B customer is the depth and complexity of the relationship. While a dissatisfied individual customer can switch service providers with relative ease, not so a B2B customer. (This is sometimes referred to as a "sticky" relationship.)

Going back to the example of large investment management firms and their custodial bank, it's extremely hard, costly, and time-consuming to change custodial banks. This can be both good and bad for both parties. It means a failing provider may have more time to recover from customer dissatisfaction and mend a relationship. It can be good for the B2B customer since they enjoy considerable leverage and can use it to get concessions and influence the service provider's operation. Being in a deep and complex relationship can be bad for both parties because problems can become endemic and acrimony between the provider and the customer can become severe and potentially do long-term damage to both parties.

It should be noted that some companies (e.g., airlines, credit card companies) attempt (and are often successful) at being "sticky" by offering value-added "reward points" and similar incentives to increase individual and even B2B customer loyalty. But it must be remembered that even the stickiest of relationships can be dissolved if customer dissatisfaction is profound and lasting.

Other Customers

Literally anyone can have the attributes of a customer. For example, the security guard who manages employee access to the work setting can be a customer. The guard can feel satisfied or dissatisfied with individual or groups of employees and can act accordingly. If the guard is acknowledged and treated in a polite and friendly manner, they may be more willing to assist an employee if there's a problem. If the guard is treated disrespectfully, or simply ignored, the guard may be unwilling to help, or to help only reluctantly. Likewise, custodial or housekeeping personnel are both customers and providers. These people are often virtually invisible to other employees in their organization. Feeling invisible can be demeaning and lead to support staff acting in a manner reflecting their dissatisfaction (e.g., putting in minimal effort in certain areas). These are only two examples. There are many examples of potentially invisible coworkers (e.g., cafeteria personnel, building maintenance staff, even IT Help Desk personnel).

> *We are all surrounded by customers,* by people who can feel satisfied or dissatisfied with our behavior or performance and act based on that satisfaction or dissatisfaction. Students are customers of their teachers and vice versa, patients are customers of their healthcare provider, communities and community members are customers of local government, local and state governments are customers of the Federal government, and the list goes on.

An Important Caveat

In the preceding examples, the satisfied and dissatisfied customer, internal or external, *can* act in a manner reflecting their satisfaction or dissatisfaction. The operative word here is *"can."* It's a probability, not a certainty. For example, an employee who is dissatisfied with their supervisor *may not* act out their dissatisfaction by being unmotivated, unproductive, or quitting. Instead, they may have a strong work ethic and perform in an exemplary manner no matter how dissatisfied they are with their supervisor. Thus, all the preceding examples are expressions of likelihood. This in no way diminishes the inclusive definition of customer. Nor does it diminish the importance of satisfying the myriad of customers that surround all of us.

Summary

Imagine a series of concentric circles. In the center is the customer (internal or external to the provider organization) making the service request and the individual employee, work group, or organization that took the original request. Extending out from the center, both immediately and over time, is every other individual or organizational entity that directly or indirectly has experience with the request or downstream consequence of the request. It is not an exaggeration to suggest that the numbers of circles extending from the center are potentially enumerable, though not unlimited. For an extreme example, my grandmother may have requested service from a given service provider years ago. If her experience was extraordinarily good or bad, it may become a family myth—with all the exaggeration inherent in myths—and thus, I hear about it as I become a customer and it shapes my expectations.

While the configuration of concentric circles is a useful image, it may be too "clean." A better metaphor might be a pond with multiple ripples interacting with one another, each affecting and being affected by other ripples. In many instances, the service experience is non-linear. It's messy, nuanced, and at every point internal or external customer satisfaction will rise or fall.

Discussed next is the basic "geography" of the customer service organization. Understanding the nature of all kinds of customers (e.g., end customers, B2B customers, internal customer) combined with an understanding of the typical service organization moves us closer to defining what customers want and the resources arrayed to deliver service to the customer in a way that drives satisfaction and (as will be discussed later) even customer loyalty.

What are the Ingredients of a Customer Service Organization?

People

Obviously, people are critical to client service. Even in a service setting that is highly automated, people are in the service mix to handle exceptions, VIP customers, internal customers, service problems, etc. People are often the focus for praise or blame when service is exemplary or when problems occur. (However, as will be discussed later, most service problems occur because of flawed work processes.)

It should also be understood that much of what the customer receives from their service provider is expected. For example, customers expect the people serving them to be provided with accurate information; however, since accuracy is an expected outcome, customer satisfaction does not rise with an accurate service delivery. However, if the customer experiences an error, customer dissatisfaction will often be the result (as discussed earlier, the B2B customer may, at least for a while, be an exception). We get angry about the error. Along with other causes, people do make mistakes that produce errors.

Customers want the people providing service to be polite, friendly, and professional. The customer wants the people providing service to be good listeners. Customers judge the behavior of the people providing customer service. If customers judge the behavior of the person providing service negatively (e.g., the service representative is rude, sarcastic, uses an unfriendly tone), the customer may become dissatisfied to very dissatisfied. By contrast, if the service provider's behavior is judged positively (e.g., genuine politeness, empathic listening), customers may be satisfied or very satisfied. Thus, while some service attributes are expected (e.g., 100% accuracy) and won't drive satisfaction up, other service attributes such as provider behavior, can work in either direction—driving satisfaction down because of perceived poor behavior or up because of effective behaviors (e.g., friendly, polite, empathic listening).

In most contemporary customer service operations, the individual service provider (employee) is not delivering information or data in a straight line (i.e., reading numbers off a screen and repeating them verbatim to the customer). Instead, they are often *interpreting* multiple data points and then providing a response to the customer. For example, the doctor looks at multiple test results to formulate a treatment plan. When the delivery of the results of multiple data points requires one or more calculations, the inevitability of a service problem increases in direct relationship to the number of calculations. Even when data is delivered in a "straight line"—reading the number off a screen—problems may still occur. The number may be wrong because of a keystroke error, the person providing customer service may read the number wrong or incomplete, or the customer may hear the number "wrong." (Even in the last case, the service provider will most likely be blamed.)

There is no "grand fix" for service delivery problems of the people variety. Obviously, rigorous selection methods, training, professional development, timely support, performance monitoring, effective supervision, useful technology, and monitoring are all part of the known answer. However, one of the fixes is to treat contemporary customer service for what it really is: a complex process with a lot of moving parts. Among these moving parts, as mentioned earlier, is customer wants versus needs. It takes a fairly sophisticated and well-trained service person to discriminate wants versus needs, especially when the customer doesn't understand or agree with the separation. Thus, contemporary customer service providers no longer need clerks or single function service representatives; instead, they need "pilots and navigators." They need people who can see beyond their literal and figurative cubicle. They need people who understand the difference between wants and needs, and who can ensure that needs are always met and wants addressed, if possible. Service providers need people who can interpret and provide the *meaning* behind the often-bewildering amount and complexity of information.

Service organizations also need people with the "right" behavioral skills. As asserted earlier, everyone is surrounded by customers, so everyone needs *at least* basic interpersonal skills. Everyone needs to be able to listen to their customer and provide information that is clear and useful. For those employees interacting with end-customers, especially sophisticated customers, more advanced interpersonal skills are needed (e.g., negotiating, real-time problem solving, empathic listening). Unfortunately, the delivery of behavioral skills training is often poorly addressed, if addressed at all. For example, we can all agree that front-line physicians (GPs, ER doctors) need good-to-superior interpersonal skills. At the same time, in healthcare (and most other professions) systemic training in interpersonal skills is seldom viewed as hierarchically equivalent to technical skills—not even close.

Even if we make all the right moves with the people-side of service delivery, there will still be people-related service errors. But if employees are selected effectively, well trained, given the tools they need for the job, compensated fairly, and managed well, people-related problems can be minimized. However, as discussed in what follows, many (perhaps most) of what is initially viewed as human error finds its roots in the work process.

Process

The second contributing cause to customer service effectiveness or ineffectiveness is the work process itself. Even if the people perform perfectly, if they are working with a flawed process, the outcome of their work will inevitably be flawed to some degree. Two of the early founders of the service quality movement, W. Edwards Deming and Joseph M. Juran, performed significant (peer reviewed) research in support of the assertion that better than 80% of all quality delivery problems are the result of flawed work process.[*]

---

[*] "A Note on Quality: The Views of Deming, Juran, and Crosby," Copyright 1986 by the President and Fellows of Harvard College.

The process does not get flawed by itself—it has help. The simple passage of time contributes to flawed process. Once a process is put in place, it begins to interact with older processes and with the ebb and flow of daily requirements. While we typically look at process as a set of steps leading to an outcome, most work processes are more like an additional layer on a huge layer cake. As soon as we put the layer on, it begins to affect and be affected by the rest of the "cake". This layering and the resulting interactions with other processes and forces creates instability and unpredictability. From instability and unpredictability come service problems.

Process Flaw (albeit archaic) Leading to Errors

In the mid '90s, I was asked by one of my customers to figure out why recurring errors were happening in a transaction processing operation. I found that the form used to initiate the transaction (based on a customer phone request) had 3 pages, the latter 2 being a copy of page 1. The person taking the request and using the form was told/trained to print clearly and to bear down a bit, "You're making 2 copies." The first page was retained (filed) by customer service, the second was sent to the compliance area, and the third page was sent to the data entry area. The third page was the least legible of the 3 pages, but it was used to enter the transaction detail, and that's where the errors were happening, not because of a human error, but because the process was flawed.

In addition to time and inter-process interaction, people inevitably alter the work process, intentionally and unintentionally. There is a difference (usually) in the design of a work process and the practical application of the process. It looks good on paper, and then the day-to-day reality of the workplace asserts itself. People create "work-arounds." Often, with the best of intentions, they figure out what they think is a better way to do "it" (whatever "it" happens to be). They often do the workaround on the fly. They don't tell anyone, they don't consider the implications, they just do it. The workaround may be exactly the right thing to do, but if it's not systematically integrated into a repeatable process, it can still create serious service problems.

Another contributor to error takes place in the design phase. As stated above, most processes start out okay. But some don't. Some are wrong from the beginning. The process may have been designed by someone without any firsthand experience of the work environment in which the process will be deployed. The process designer(s) thought they

[23]

knew enough, or they may have thought that they didn't need to know about the work environment, and they had the authority to design process or make process changes. The combination of authority and ignorance is always dangerous.

> It is beyond the purview of this discussion, but some mention must be made of Just-in-Time (JIT), a supply chain work process that moves manufacturing materials (or information) just before they are needed. During the pandemic, we experienced huge disruptions in the supply chain. JIT is a process ill-equipped to respond to an unanticipated global crisis. In turn, this affects accuracy of projections between suppliers, their business customers, and the end customer. This illustrates a largely unanticipated process failure, but a failure that remains unaddressed, since process is typically not designed around exceptional circumstances. However, what we have seen lately is the exceptional becoming the "new normal."

The work process can contribute to problems, or it can fail to contribute to effective service. The reasons and potential reasons for the failure are legion. The root cause for bad process might be one of the examples cited above, or one of many others. Usually process failure is the result of interacting forces. The process can be designed properly, and existing process can be fixed, but it's literally a continuous challenge to do so.

There are two major ways to fix the existing work process—*process improvement* and *process reengineering*. Process improvement refers to actions taken to "tweak" the current work process to make it work better. Reengineering on the other hand, involves creating brand new processes from (at least symbolically) a "blank sheet of paper." Process improvement is like taking your car in for a major tune-up. Reengineering is like driving your car off a cliff, hoping you'll survive the crash, and buying a new and different car.

From a cost benefit and risk standpoint, process improvement makes a lot of sense. Incremental process improvements can be made at a relatively low cost and risk. However, if the core process or reasoning behind the process is flawed in some major and fundamental way, reengineering may be called for. Reengineering represents a fundamental change. Fundamental change can be exactly the right thing to do, but it takes time and expertise, and brings cost and, potentially, increased risk.

Business process improvement and reengineering are major "fronts" in improving service delivery across virtually every service setting. If the process is improved or reengineered into a "perfect" state, the opportunity and the probability for error goes down. Importantly, improving a process doesn't reduce service problems to zero now and forever, it reduces the probability of error.

The formal techniques for creating and improving a business process have been around since the early 20th century and have proven validity.* With each iteration, there is a risk of process improvement or reengineering having faddish attributes. The faddishness comes from the people involved in the improvement process. All too often, they are consultants or internal people who share a common and fatal flaw: they are committed to their particular "brand" of process creation or improvement. They may, unintentionally, value form over function. They may be sycophants of one of the current crop of management gurus, or they may think of themselves as an emerging guru. These can be dangerous people, creating unnecessary divisions between individuals and groups. These same people tend to use jargon rather than commonly understood words. They want to "drill down" versus look at a problem in detail. They want to "un-pack" the situation or problem. They want to "think outside the box" to get the "low hanging fruit" and they may want to take the conversation "offline" to find "leverage." They want to create "synergies" instead of simply saying they need to encourage teamwork. And for some reason, they are concerned about what's in and outside of the "wheelhouse" (as if we are on board a 19th century whaling vessel).

> The irony of criticizing jargon and, at the same time, using the abbreviation WACW, is not lost on me. The offset to this contradiction is to make every effort to use clear and unambiguous language and, wherever possible, use concrete examples and analogies.

Another problem with process improvement is that it can be very complex and difficult to implement. The tools for creation, improvement, and reengineering are hard to deploy, difficult to manage, and tricky to interpret. Also, any improvement or reengineering effort

---

* "Frederick Taylor's Principles of Scientific Management Theory," Ward, Patrick, NanoGlobals (online), 2021

that focuses myopically on the work process is doomed unless it recognizes that any one process interacts with other processes, depends on people, and has to be supported by enabling technology.

While there is clear, intended, and unapologetic criticism of jargon and cults expressed here and elsewhere in this book, it has to be acknowledged that some business process reengineering and improvement tools are unquestionably effective. For example, Lean Six Sigma, a process tool that, among other outcomes, removes "waste" and decreases process variation, has a proven record of success.[*] Even in this example however, there is a danger of Lean Six Sigma becoming, among practitioners, a kind of business cult, where people are either true believers or not. (The advent of "belts" signifying a level of proficiency in Lean Six Sigma is a bit troubling.)

Even when process improvement or reengineering works, service delivery problems will still occur, errors will still happen; but with an optimized, integrated process, problems will be minimized. In terms of return on investment, and even with all the complexity and challenges, service organizations will get a high return from investing in almost continuous process monitoring and improvement aimed at optimizing the customer service process.

Technology

The third contributing cause of effective and ineffective customer service is technology. Technology has changed our experience of the world in general and of customer service in particular. Technology has enabled gains in quality and productivity in virtually every part of customer service organization. A single customer service employee with the right enabling technology can do the work that multiple employees did just a few decades ago (and it might be a high multiple, depending on the service job). It's the same for customers. With the right technology, customers can engage in simple to quite complex self-service.

A prime example of self-service technology is the ATM. As long ago as the 1970s, ATMs became part of the customer service landscape. Instead of going to the bank and being served by a teller, the customer

---

[*] "5 Success Stories of Lean (Six) Sigma Implementation," Amile Institute (2021)

can go to the nearest ATM to make withdrawals, deposits, and transfers, among other more complex transactions. Coming forward to the present day, I can use my computer to access and receive services from a myriad of service organizations, from banking and insurance, to buying movie tickets online, or accessing my social security account. Today, I can do all of this with my hand-held device, from anywhere, at any time.

New and emerging technologies can drive satisfaction up sharply—even causing customer delight. (People queuing up for hours to get the latest iPhone is only one piece of evidence for the power of new technology.) However, after a relatively brief period, even the most transformative technologies become *expected*. Again, think about the ATM. When ATMs first came out, for many customers they were a wonder, driving satisfaction up for the service provider (Citi Bank in the late '70s and early '80s). Come forward into the 21st century and in 2016, there were an estimated 2.5+ million ATMs worldwide. (The number of ATMs may peak and begin to drop off with the increase in cashless payment systems.) At this point, and arguably for the past couple of decades, customers expect an ATM to work and when it does, it simply meets the customer's expectation but does not raise their satisfaction. By contrast, if the ATM is offline or doesn't work, or one is not nearby, the customer will be dissatisfied, perhaps deeply dissatisfied.

There are many ways that technology has fostered improved customer service. Requests that used to take days or weeks to handle can now be addressed in minutes via self-service or during a single phone call with a customer service representative (CSR) using enabling technology. Errors and timeliness issues arising from manual processing (e.g., in banking, insurance) have been significantly reduced. Technology can also solve and often eliminate process problems. It can "force" the user down a path of proper, effective procedural steps (process) versus having service employees or their customers follow procedures manually. Technology can eliminate unnecessary or inefficient decision making via rules-based decision trees.

What technology does best is access and handle a large volume of data/information much faster and more accurately than people can. An effective customer service provider can leverage technology's fundamental strength to enable individual or B2B customer service providers to focus on engaging with their customer, really listening, and building a relationship. (**Note:** One of the recent buzz words/ phrases one often hears in business is "relationship selling," which means, among other things, building a partnership with the sales prospect. It may be a strategically good idea to use technology to foster so-called "relationship service.")

Obviously, there are problems with customer service technology. System outages can cripple an entire business enterprise. It seems that weekly we hear about malware or ransomware, each of which can cause both immediate and lasting harm to the customer service organization and its customers. Phishing, in which bad actors masquerading as reputable companies, trick individuals into providing private information, and is on the rise. Passwords are a continuing source of irritation and frustration for both service providers and their customers. Yes, there are automated systems in place to retain and use passwords, but heaven help you if you need to change your settings or use a new service and don't have your passwords written down somewhere. Two factor authorization, in which you need both your password and a single use number sent to your cell phone, can also be tedious and frustrating, especially if you're in a hurry. Both passwords and two-factor authorization are pure examples of the phrase, "necessary evils." With the increased use of biometric technologies (e.g., facial, fingerprint, or voice recognition) we may begin to see the end of the era of passwords. However, if the past is a predictor of the future, unanticipated problems with biometrics will emerge.

We are living in a time when the label "Artificial Intelligence (AI)" is in ubiquitous use, but it's fair to question whether artificial intelligence is a reality. Are even our most advanced computer systems truly intelligent? Are our computers even close to equivalent to an organic brain and its ability to perceive the environment and act in a way that maximizes goal achievement? Will quantum computers bridge the cognitive gap between a machine and an intelligent machine? These questions, while fascinating, are beyond the purview of this discussion, except to say that emerging technologies, especially AI, will change customer service. It's also fair to say that some of those changes will be good and some bad, from both the customer's and the provider's perspective.

Added to technology problems affecting customer service, some experience deleterious health effects [as a secondary effect of some technology and technology use]. Excessive screen time, screen glare, poor sitting posture, and even depression have all been linked to the use of technology (e.g., desktop systems, laptops, handheld devices)[*]. An entire scientific discipline (ergonomics) is devoted, in part, to how people work in their environment. If a generalization can be permitted, it's simply not a good idea to have 6 to 8 hours or more of screen time every day. This obviously applies to the client-facing service representative at, for example, a telephone contact center. It also affects anyone using technology to do their job, which, more than two decades into the 21st century, is *a lot* of people.

Where does technology go right or go wrong? It can go right or wrong at any point in the technology development and deployment process, from initial planning to design or coding and testing. However, ask most IT people or their business clients and many (perhaps most) will say that the single most important step in the development lifecycle is the requirements gathering phase. It is during requirements gathering that the technology development experts work with the ultimate users (e.g., internal customers) of the new technology. In my own experience and on many more than one occasion, I've experienced fundamental antipathy between the technology experts and their users. Users think the IT people don't really understand the business and IT people likewise think that users don't really understand technology. All too often, both are correct. That's why successful development lifecycles, producing effective customer service tools, focus on exhaustive user input gathering conducted by people with strong interpersonal skills, especially listening skills, as well as expertise in process analysis and documentation. Also useful are some of the more formal, time-tested models for the development lifecycle (e.g., the standardized SDLC-Software Development Lifecycle-model, IBM's Agile approach).

****

---

[*] Tucker, Frank "Top 10 Computer Related Health Problems," June 15, 2016, @2019 Microhealth LLC, Vienna, VA.

Up to this point, two base-laying concepts have been presented and discussed. The first concept is that *a customer is anyone in a position to feel satisfied or dissatisfied about what you (the service provider) do, and the customer is able to act based on their satisfaction or dissatisfaction.* The second concept is defining the structure of the customer service organization as consisting of three interdependent elements: People, Process, and Technology.

At this point, the discussion will move to the specifics of what the customer wants from their service provider. Moving forward, each of the components of What All Customers Want (WACW) will be defined, illustrated with prescriptive examples, and the connection of each WACW component with all the other components will be described.

There are six components of WACW:

1. Accuracy
2. Timeliness
3. Access
4. Utility
5. Responsiveness
6. Problem Recovery

Before going into detail about each element of WACW, two clarifying points need to be made.

1. No Hierarchy

There is no hierarchy, no element of WACW that is *always* more important than the others. While it's always tempting to force a list of attributes into a certain order, it would not only be wrong to do so, but it would also compromise the ability to understand, apply, and achieve WACW.

The above being said, there can be a *situational* hierarchy to the element of WACW. For example, in a specific customer service situation in which all the elements are present at an expected or satisfying level, but there's a problem with access, then access becomes the most important influencer of customer satisfaction or dissatisfaction. Likewise, with all the other elements, or grouping of elements, if it or they become problematic, they rise *situationally* in the hierarchy.

2. Satisfiers and Dissatisfiers

It's worth noting again that some of the elements of WACW are expected and even when delivered effectively, they will not produce satisfaction or a rise in satisfaction. Instead, these elements can be described as "dissatisfiers" since when there's a problem (e.g., an error), they typically only engender low to very low satisfaction. For example, I call my bank to get my balance, and I am given my balance. This does not produce satisfaction, much less rising satisfaction. I got what I expected. In stark contrast, if I call my bank to get my balance and am told it is not available, or the amount I'm given is incorrect, now I'm dissatisfied to very dissatisfied.[*]

So, what is a satisfier? Interestingly, two elements of WACW can drive satisfaction or, more correctly, can work in both directions: Responsiveness and Problem Recovery. For example, a customer calls their service provider's contact center. The Customer Service Representative (CSR) is polite, demonstrates a positive tone, speaks plainly, and clearly listens and demonstrates an understanding of the customer's questions or concerns. The customer's experience with the CSR's behavior is very satisfying, and importantly, that satisfaction does not diminish with repeated exposure to the CSR with effective communication skills. The customer always likes to be served by a provider with superior interpersonal skills, especially one who listens, and demonstrates empathy.

Somewhat ironically, Effective Problem Recovery can also be a satisfier. For example, the customer has one of his shirts damaged by the dry cleaner. Instead of simply apologizing or arguing with the customer over the value of the shirt, the dry cleaner buys the customer a brand new, identical shirt. The customer is very satisfied and may become a loyal customer as well as recommend others to the dry cleaner. And, by the way, the cost of buying the new shirt is very low, compared to the long-term gain from a loyal customer. (In the interest of disclosure and transparency, this happened to me.) Of course, this example falls apart if the dry cleaner routinely ruins customer's garments. It should also be understood that poor

---

[*] The concept of satisfiers and dissatisfiers comes from the work by Frederic Hertzberg in the 1950s. He applied the concept to employee motivation, specifically Motivating Factors (Satisfiers) and Hygiene Factors (dissatisfiers).

problem recovery, which is all too prevalent, often leads to a dissatisfied to very dissatisfied customer.

It would be easier to explain and understand WACW if each element was exclusively a satisfier or a dissatisfier. Accuracy, timeliness, access, and utility *tend* to be dissatisfiers, but not always. For example, a new means of access, like the evolution of new technologies to access service, can early in their rollout, drive satisfaction. But a new means of access will quickly become the expected means of access and long-term, the failure of that access technology will drive dissatisfaction. By contrast, Responsiveness and Problem Recovery can work in both directions over the long term, as illustrated earlier (and in later chapters).

In and of itself, each concept presented in this chapter is easy to understand (i.e., everyone is a customer and organizations are composed of people, processes, and technology). However, when each concept is described in relation to every other concept, including the customer and what every customer wants, things get complicated. This complexity is exactly why it's important to think critically about how these concepts work, work together, and function within a customer service environment.

To provide the "ammunition" for such critical thinking, we'll move on to a detailed discussion of each component of what all ki
nds of customers want from all kinds of service providers and linking these components back to the structure of the service organization.

> *Seek the degree of precision that the*
> *subject matter will allow.*
>> —Aristotle

> *"It's good enough for government work."*
>> —Modern Proverb

Chapter 2

Accuracy

*A customer is anyone in a position to feel satisfied or dissatisfied about **accuracy** and can act based on their satisfaction or dissatisfaction.*

Accuracy is obviously and unarguably a critical component in the delivery of customer service. At first glance, accuracy seems easy to define. It is correct information, data, or guidance. Accuracy is the absence of error. However, thinking more deeply about accuracy in different contexts, the definition becomes more complex.

Accuracy is an *expected* outcome of service delivery. This means that when the customer receives accurate information or data, their satisfaction typically does not rise. They expected accuracy and they got it. However, if an error occurs, it will often drive dissatisfaction. Thus, accuracy is a "dissatisfier" since there typically is no up-side to being correct, only a downside for being wrong—sometimes a significant downside, up to and including losing the customer and the customer becoming a negative voice to other customers or on social media.

> **An Exception:** If the service provider (especially the B2B service provider) has had repetitive errors and then delivers accurate information/data, it may generate satisfaction, but it will do so only briefly before accuracy again becomes expected.

There are several ways to define and describe Accuracy:

- Precision Accuracy
- Accurate Enough
- Accuracy as the Truth
- An Individual Customer's Experience of Accuracy
- Normative Accuracy for B2B Customers

Precision Accuracy

As the term implies, precision accuracy is strict and exact. It is most often the delivery of data from the service provider to the customer. For example, I call my bank for a balance in one of my savings accounts and a service representative provides me with a specific number, say, "$1,262.57 at the close of business on X date." The service representative does not say, "you have a little over twelve hundred dollars."

Taking precision accuracy further, a large investment company requesting financial data from its bank—in a B2B relationship—can reasonably expect the bank to provide a very high level of precision when reporting amounts (e.g., dollar amounts, number of shares). If the bank is reporting dollar amounts, it will report out to two decimal places (just like my bank reporting on my savings account). However, if the bank is reporting on the number of shares held or the current value of a given security, the bank might report out to five or six decimal places because of the large number of shares, or the fact that the bank is processing millions of transactions every day. Interestingly, in the case of cyber currency like Bitcoin, the bank may report out to 50 decimal places or more because of the extremely high volume and value extending to the right of the decimal point.

> Thinking about accuracy/error rates, a 1% or less accuracy rate sounds good until you put some real numbers to the equation. For example, it is not uncommon for a large custody bank to process transactions valued at millions of dollars every day. If the bank touts a 99% accuracy rate, which does sound good, customers must remember that 1% of 1,000,000 is 10,000. That's 10,000 mistakes. And while subjective, for the customer experiencing an error, the error rate is 100%.

We might also think about precision accuracy within the context of other, very technical professions. For example, a neurosurgeon who is close to accurate, but not precisely accurate, can produce catastrophic results for their patients (customers). Similarly, a ship's captain needs a focus on precision accuracy. A ship sailing from New York to London that is off course by even a few degrees might end up in North Africa. Examples abound across an array of settings from insurance and banking to airlines and hospitals. In all these settings, there is an expectation for precision accuracy. In other settings, however, precision/perfect accuracy is not required, as described next.

Accurate Enough

I call my service provider and request that certain information be sent to me via the U.S. postal service (for example, a document with a raised seal). The service representative stipulates that the document in question will be sent out at the close of business (today) and that I should receive it in 7 to 10 business days. This is an example of "accurate enough." (Later, I'll use this same example when discussing timeliness.) The service representative can specify a range, but not a specific day and time, nor do they need to, to be accurate enough. If the customer needs greater precision, they can request next-day delivery by companies such as FedEx, UPS, or the U.S. postal service. However, even there, the service representative won't be able to specify the hour and minute of delivery. A useful image to illustrate the concept of accurate enough is the classic bell curve. The absolute peak of the bell represents precision accuracy, but moving a few degrees off the peak will, in many instances, be accurate enough. (The word "enough" in the context of this discussion means enough to address the customer's need or service request. Enough is "fit for use.")

A doctor prescribing a broad-spectrum antibiotic (e.g., Doxycycline, Ampicillin) is likely to be accurate enough. The medication targets a wide range of disease-causing bacteria.

A pilot landing on an airport does not need to be perfectly aligned to the exact center of the runway. Clearly, the pilot can only be a few inches off the center to avoid a potential catastrophe, but looking at a photograph of a runway, one can clearly see skid marks to the right and left of the exact, precise center of the runway.

> At the risk of going down a rabbit hole, it should be acknowledged that most of us are customers of an array of media outlets (e.g., TV, radio, internet). Two plus decades into the 21st century, the truth has become suspect. Two ideologically opposed media outlets are likely to present two opposing perceptions of what is true. Both will support their version of the truth with data, expert opinions, and even video/audio recordings. Both will interpret the data, select experts, and interpret recordings to suit their underlying ideology.
>
> In turn, Customers can select their media outlet to suit and support their ideological world view. It is possible to find outlets that present
>
> Continued →

[35]

peer reviewed and valid science, credentialed and credible experts, and make a concerted effort to reduce or eliminate bias; but as time goes by, the rational seems to be losing ground to the ideological. The truth is losing ground to the lie.

Some will bristle at the concept of accurate enough. They want precision accuracy in all service encounters. While this may sound right, the cost and complexity of achieving perfect accuracy in all service deliveries is at once unnecessary and almost impossible to achieve.

Accuracy as the Truth

Precision accuracy and accurate enough are also truthful. Customers of all kinds want and expect their service provider to be truthful. As the customer of my supervisor or manager, I expect my supervisor or manager to tell me the truth about my performance and career opportunities. If I'm a supervisor, and thus a customer of my employee, I expect my employee to tell me the truth when describing an event or situation. So too the external customer. Everyone wants the truth from everyone else.

But the truth can be tricky. I want my financial advisor to tell me the truth about risk, but it is in no one's interest to overstate the risk factors inherent in almost any investment. The critically or chronically ill patient wants the truth from their physician, but not necessarily the truth bereft of any hope, however slight.

The truth is more subjective than precision accuracy or accurate enough. The truth or untruth is delivered via language, either written or verbal, with the inherent attribute of tone. Thus, even a completely true statement, delivered in vague language or a tone that conveys uncertainty, can be perceived as untrue or less than fully true. Likewise, a lie (untruth), delivered with concrete and specific language with a confident tone, may be perceived as true.

Furthermore, whether the information given to the customer is true or false may only be discoverable after a period of time. Going back to the example of the financial advisor, the truth or falseness of the advisor's advice and approach can only be judged after months, or even years of experience. In a more classic setting, a customer receiving information from a telephone service representative, the discovery of the truth or falseness of the representative's statement will probably happen within hours or days.

A lie or less than fully true statement will, when discovered, drive customer dissatisfaction, potentially extreme dissatisfaction. The truth is expected, even demanded. However, because of the inherent "packaging" (e.g., words used and tone), the truth, delivered effectively, even artfully, may drive increased customer satisfaction, even sustained satisfaction (i.e., the customer grows to like the truth-teller). However, the "fall from grace" can be quick and steep in the event of a lie or less than a fully true presentation. For example, if I find out that my doctor, who I had previously judged as a truth-teller, has lied to me or withheld information I needed, my dissatisfaction may be fast, profound, and lasting.

A final note about the truth as an element of WACW: Just like fight or flight is seemingly hardwired into our makeup, so too we *may* be hardwired to lie after having made a mistake for which the consequences are dire, extending all the way to termination. Holding on to and prospering on a job can be likened to survival and prospering in the natural world. Certainly, this assertion can be questioned and even dismissed as too extreme or unproven. The point here is that a person who makes an error may, almost immediately, deny culpability, hide the error, or blame someone else—sometimes even the customer. As an offset to this possibility, the effective service provider tries to create a work environment that encourages—even rewards— accountability. The obvious exception to the practice of rewarding accountability occurs when the service employee makes repetitive errors at a number above or well above the standard of performance. In this situation, even if the employee takes accountability, remediation must occur (e.g., retraining, transferring, or even termination).

An Individual Customer's Experience of Accuracy and Errors

While individual and B2B customers (businesses served by or serving other businesses) want perfect, 100% accuracy, they don't necessarily expect it. We have all experienced error and we've all made mistakes.

For an individual customer experiencing an error, dissatisfaction is likely but not inevitable. There are several dependencies. What's the magnitude of the error? Large, high magnitude errors are more likely to produce dissatisfaction than relatively small or minor errors. Is it a single error or only the latest in a series of mistakes? A single error of relatively small magnitude is less likely to engender dissatisfaction than a pattern of errors, or, even worse, a pattern of high magnitude errors. How well or poorly did the provider recover from the errors? An entire chapter will be devoted to problem recovery; but sufficed to say here, effective, aggressive problem recovery can reduce customer dissatisfaction and even push its way into satisfaction and even loyalty, while poor problem recovery is likely to increase dissatisfaction, potentially by a lot.

The individual customer's experience of error is different than a B2B customer's experience. Even if the service provider has a 99.5% accuracy rate, the individual customer suffering an error may experience a 100% error rate (as stated earlier), especially if they are an infrequent user of the provider and it's a high magnitude error.

Normative Accuracy for B2B Customers

Institutional customers are different. The B2B customer is being serviced by a B2B service provider. The B2B customer's perception of accuracy is an aggregated view of all service deliveries both to the B2B customer itself and, often, to the B2B customer's customer. When assessing the service provider, the B2B customer is looking for *normative* accuracy—*the extent to which the service provider's accuracy rate compares favorably to other B2B service providers.* The institutional customer and their service provider accept the reality that some, albeit small, error rate is inevitable. Thus, the customer will not be dissatisfied if the provider delivers accurate information/data at a level equal to or greater than other providers. If the service provider delivers at an accuracy rate greater than other providers, the customer may experience a rise in satisfaction, but only temporarily, since the higher accuracy rate will soon (in weeks or months) become the expected level of accuracy. The B2B customer's customer (the end-customer) can be a "wild-card" disrupting the concept of normative accuracy. If the end-customer experiences an error, or a pattern of error, they may complain to their provider, the B2B customer. Depending on the perceived importance of the end-customer, their complaint (even though accuracy rates in general are at or above the norm) may be disproportionately important to the B2B customer. Another factor that can disrupt the concept of normative accuracy is social media. For example, a single end-customer experiencing a single error might have a Twitter following or Facebook (Meta) friends numbering into the thousands, or even tens of thousands. If this customer voices dissatisfaction on social media, it can produce outcomes wildly out of proportion to the error. The service provider may be forced to take action that is both costly and which ultimately has little impact of normative accuracy. It may even have a negative impact on, for example, the morale of the provider's service team employees.

Accuracy In Relation to the Other Elements of What All Customers Want (WACW)

Accuracy and Timeliness: Late information or data is almost by definition, inaccurate. Timeliness and accuracy are inextricably linked. A clear example of the link is when precision or perfect accuracy is required. In this case, if the precisely accurate information or data is provided late, it can be judged as inaccurate. For another example, if the customer wants to purchase company stock at a specific price and is given old or late (stale) pricing information, the price given to the customer can be judged as not only late, but also incorrect. The customer's decisions based on late information/data will be flawed and may be costly. Similarly, if a banking customer calls the bank's contact center and asks for a current account balance and the customer service representative (CSR) provides the balance as of the preceding day, without specifying that conditional response, the figure given can be judged as incorrect. (That's why financial service firm CSRs typically give the "as of" information in response to pricing or balance questions.)

Accuracy and Access: If the information, data, or service is inaccessible, both accuracy and timeliness become meaningless. For example, if the customer goes to an ATM and it is down (for whatever reason) then, what the customer wanted is inaccessible. The provider being accessible or inaccessible is not limited to technology-mediated customer service. If the customer calls their provider and the wait time is excessive, or the prompt menus are perceived as onerous to the customer, this can be another example of access being denied. Obviously, the two negative examples can be reversed to show positive access and accuracy. For example, the customer goes to the ATM and can almost immediately get an accurate account balance and makes a withdrawal; or the customer has almost immediate access to the provider's call center.

> While working as a consultant to several large transaction/data processing providers, I had direct experience with end-customers as "wild cards." Murphy's Law (i.e., if anything can go wrong, it will, and at the most inopportune time) seemed to kick in just before an annual meeting between the provider and their B2B customer. In several instances, a member of the customer's Board of Directors experienced an error. The Board member complained to the B2B customer about the B2B service provider. Then, instead of focusing on critical business issues and decisions, a good bit of the annual meeting was focused on a single error from among literally *millions* of transactions. As an aside, one way I knew I was dealing with a superior senior executive was the extent to which they could move the focus from the incidental "noise" to issues of real strategic importance.

Accuracy and Usefulness: If the customer receives service that is not useful the way the customer wanted to use it, the service could be judged as inaccurate precisely because it is not useful. For example, if the customer requests electronic delivery of certain information or data in a particular format or application version, and the provider sends the information in a different format or version, the customer can't use it. It doesn't matter if the information or data is accurate and timely, if the information isn't useful, it's no good to the customer.

Accuracy and Responsiveness: Responsiveness can be defined in several ways. It's defined here as the behavior of the service provider (as a company, or as the provider's representative). On an individual level, the client service representative (CSR) responsiveness behavior is a function of, among other behaviors, genuine politeness, tone, clarity, loudness, and the CSR's ability to listen to the customer and respond in a way that demonstrates understanding. An example of the interaction of accuracy and responsiveness is when the CSR speaks too quickly, is abrupt/terse, dismissive, or claims to understand without demonstrating understanding *but is also providing accurate information or data*. The customer in this case may be generally dissatisfied with the CSR's behavior *and* question or doubt the accuracy of the CSR's response. In contrast, the CSR demonstrates effective behavior but provides inaccurate information or data. The customer in this case accepts the CSR's response as correct because it was delivered in a confident tone of voice. Obviously, the best combination is effective communication behavior and an accurate response. The point here is that behavior can profoundly affect the customer's perception of accuracy and inaccuracy.

Accuracy and Problem Recovery: Obviously, the customer receiving inaccurate information will be dissatisfied. However, if the error is acknowledged in a timely manner and then subject to effective, even aggressive problem recovery, the customer's dissatisfaction will probably be lessened. In fact, as will be discussed later, effective problem recovery can drive satisfaction and even loyalty. Service providers and their representatives *define their true nature and culture by how they respond to the inevitable service problems.* In stark contrast, if the customer experiences an error and the provider fails to acknowledge the problem, becomes argumentative, and/or fails to recover effectively, there are now two problems: the error and the failure to recover effectively.

Some Examples of Accuracy for Certain Types of Customers

What follows is a table enumerating some specific types of accuracy related to certain customers and their service provider. This is *not* an exhaustive list of all customer types, service providers, or types of accuracy important to the customer. These examples illustrate the diversity of customers and the types of accuracy they might expect.

Customer Type	Provider Type	Accuracy Type
Individual Customers (in general)	Service Providers	• Precision accuracy if numbers, amounts, or data are part of the service process • Accurate enough to meet the customer's request/expressed need
B2B Customer	B2B Provider	Norm References Accuracy
Financial Service End Customer	Financial Service Provider (e.g., Banks, Investment)	Precision accuracy to at least 2 decimal places (more, depending on asset type)
Supervisor/ Manager	Employees	Performance compares favorably to others doing the same job— Norm References Accuracy
Healthcare Patient	Healthcare Provider	• Precision accuracy about test results and medication regimen • The truth about diagnosis and prognosis
Healthcare Provider	Patient	The truth about the patient experience (e.g., symptoms, habits, diet, and exercise) **Note:** The experienced provider may be able to account for exaggeration and omission.
Employee (all levels, all types)	Employee's Supervisor/ Manager	The truth about responsibilities, opportunities, performance expectations, feedback, etc.
Employee (all levels, all types)	The Provider Company/ Corporation	Total compensation (e.g., salary, benefits) compares favorably to others doing the same job in the same region and/or industry

Continued →

[42]

Customer Type	Provider Type	Accuracy Type
Client Facing Employees (CSRs)	End-Customers	• Precision accuracy regarding the information/data needed from the customer to provide service • The truth or accurate enough information about the customer's experience
Employee's Colleagues	Employee	General adherence to company rules/expectations (e.g., arrival time, breaks, quitting time)
Community Member	Local Government	• Precision accuracy regarding tax assessments • Norm-referenced accuracy regarding community services provided
Local Government	Community Member	• Precision accuracy regarding tax payments • Norm-referenced accuracy regarding use of community services
Students	Teachers	Accurate expectations for class participation and performance
Teachers	Students	Accurate adherence to expectations and the truth in completing assignments (no plagiarism, cheating)

The preceding list is, as the saying goes, "the tip of the iceberg."

A Call to Action

The best way to understand the elements of WACW is to apply it to real world circumstances. Thus, to fully understand accuracy, you can define its application to one or more of *your* customers. For example, if you are a manager of multiple teams employing multiple team members, each under the direction of one or more front-line supervisors, those supervisors are your customers. Each can feel satisfied or dissatisfied about what you do, and they can act individually or collectively based on their satisfaction or dissatisfaction.

Ask yourself, what do the front-line supervisors under your management expect/want from you in relation to accuracy? An example follows, but your own application to your own situation will be much more meaningful and useful.

Your Supervisors (as your customers) want...	You, as Manager—Behaviors/Actions
Precision Accuracy	You provide precise accuracy expectations for routine work output from each supervisor's team. For example: • The team level transaction processing accuracy rate for new account setup is 99.5% • There are 5% or less errors that are missed by quality assurance review and released to customers
The Truth	For any delays in your managerial functions involving individual supervisors (e.g., staff meetings, one-on-one feedback), you take accountability for the delay—no denial, no excuses. (**Note:** There may be a "good" reason for the delay, which you can explain, but the supervisor still experienced a delay for which you can and should take accountability.)
Accurate Enough	You set general guidelines for how each supervisor manages their team but leaves at least some of the specifics to each supervisor (you are not micromanaging).
Accurate Enough	Manager (you) establishes an expectation and supporting procedure for reporting on non-financial service problems within two hours of the occurrence of the problem.

If you are a manager doing this for yourself in relation to one or more of your internal or external customers, this is an effort that will solidify your understanding of accuracy as part of WACW. Your effort may be imperfect, however, over time it will become increasingly accurate and useful.

Now, the discussion will move on to the next element of What All Customers Want: Timeliness.

"Time is the fire in which we all burn."

—Soren to Picard

Doctor: *I've got bad news and really bad news.*
Patient: *Jeez! What's the bad news?*
Doctor: *Your test results show you have only 24 hours to live.*
Patient: *What's the really bad news?*
Doctor: *I got the test results yesterday.*

—Bad Joke

Chapter 3
Timeliness

*A customer is anyone in a position to feel satisfied or dissatisfied about **timeliness** and can act based on their satisfaction or dissatisfaction.*

Timeliness, like accuracy, is a critical element of what all customers want (WACW). And just like accuracy, at first glance, timeliness seems easy to define. Timeliness is being on time. My dry cleaner says my shirts will be ready on Tuesday after 8:00 a.m. and I pick up my shirts on Tuesday at 10:00 a.m. and judge the service I received as on time. However, as in accuracy, thinking more deeply about timeliness in different contexts and for different customers, the definition of timeliness becomes more complex.

Timeliness tends to be a dissatisfier. It's an expected attribute of the service provider so that when the customer receives timely service, their satisfaction is not likely to rise. However, if the customer's expectation is exceeded, the service delivery is faster than promised or expected, satisfaction might rise. However, unless the service is a "one-off" event, the faster delivery of service can quickly become an expectation, so that in subsequent service interactions, being on time might be perceived as late by the customer. A late service delivery or an excess of waiting time will drive dissatisfaction.

> **An Exception:** If the service provider (especially an institutional service provider) has routinely been late in delivering services, being on time may generate satisfaction, but it will do so only briefly before timeliness again becomes expected and thus a dissatisfier.

Like accuracy, there are several ways to define and describe Timeliness. Some can be characterized similarly, others very differently. This chapter presents several kinds of Timeliness:

- Precision Timeliness
- Timely Enough
- Timely as Fast or Faster
- Just in Time (JIT)

- The individual customer's experience of timeliness and managing waiting time
- Normative Timeliness for B2B Customers

Precision Timeliness

Precision timeliness is, as the term implies, strict and exact. For example, the train is expected to arrive at the station at 6:10 p.m. If the train arrives on schedule, it can be judged as meeting the timeliness expectation. If it arrives at 6:12 p.m. or at 6:08 p.m. it can be judged as late or early, respectively. These differences are a matter of a few minutes and may also be judged as inconsequential to all but the most exacting (or obsessive) customer. However, looking at these small discrepancies from the perspective of the train station or the larger network of trains in the region, even small discrepancies can add up.

Computer technology has become a game-changing tool for precision timeliness. For example, if a given service provider has information critical to customers or is offering an upgrade to an existing product or service, it may use technology to set and meet a precise timeliness expectation. The service provider tells its customers that the critical information or upgrade will be made available at 12:01 a.m. on a particular date, and using enabling technology, is able to meet this expectation precisely. This concept even extends to the entertainment industry regarding timing of a movie; for example, becoming available for streaming.

Another example of precision timeliness, also enabled by technology, is found in the investment industry. Algorithmic trading, a technology enabled process for executing preprogrammed trading (e.g., buy and sell orders) might define timeliness in micro-seconds. In fact, the financial trader's physical location can have a material effect on algorithmic trading, especially if they are using fiber optics to send and receive information and data. The closer the trader technology is to the exchange's servers, the timelier the transaction can be executed (taking advantage of the laws of physics governing the speed of light). Again, this may come down to one trader being microseconds faster than another, but if dollar amounts and trading volumes are in the millions or more, microseconds can make a huge difference in outcomes.

Most individual customers have little interest in timeliness measured in microseconds, but again, technology has led to a general rise in expectations for timeliness. For example, an individual customer loading the service provider's website may have an expectation of seconds rather than minutes.

Timely Enough

One way to define timely enough is by using a range. The service provider tells the customer they will receive a callback between 4:00 and 5:00 p.m. on a specific day/date. If the callback is within the provided range, it can be defined as being timely enough. Although, for some customers or in some situations, if the callback hasn't happened by around 4:45 p.m. or even sooner, the customer may start feeling anxious. For example, a healthcare patient waiting for critical (even life and death) test results is likely to become increasingly anxious as soon as the clock strikes 4:01 p.m. and no callback has occurred. Continuing with this example, if the provider makes the callback at 4:55 p.m., it can claim that they met the timeliness expectation and, objectively, they did. But the customer (patient) may be dissatisfied anyway. There is no perfect answer to this conundrum, but there are things the provider can do. The provider can decrease or narrow the range, promising to make the callback between 4:00 and 4:15 p.m. Narrowing the range may be impossible for some providers or in certain situations (e.g., the provider is waiting for information from a third party). However, narrowing the range whenever possible is likely to decrease dissatisfaction.

In the earlier discussion about accuracy in Chapter 2, "accurate enough" was illustrated with a classic bell curve. Timely enough can similarly be illustrated. With the peak of the curve representing precision timeliness but moving a few degrees off peak will be timely enough (i.e., sufficient timeliness to meet the customer's needs and not drive dissatisfaction).

Amazon may be the perfect example of a service provider that has mastered timely enough. Through Amazon's technology or its call centers, customers can get almost real-time delivery status and even map location of the delivery vehicle. It is not entirely improbable that, by some future date, Amazon and similar providers may be able to move from accurate enough to precision accuracy, although it is reasonable to question the practical need for most deliveries in most cases.

Timely as Fast or Faster

In the developed world at least, we are a culture that values speed—the faster the better. Interestingly, the phrase "fast food" entered the modern lexicon in the U.S. in 1951. The first fast food restaurant in the U.S. was White Castle in 1921, although in England, fish and chip shops were operating in the mid-19th century. Call centers in which customers could call their service provider directly began in the 1960s (with 1-800 service emerging in 1967). Fast forward to the present day and call centers are ubiquitous. Some call centers provide 24/7 availability. Yes, call centers provide faster service than, for example, the U.S. mail, but they can also be a source of frustration for customers calling in. Waiting on hold, having complex front-end menus, having to repeat the service request to more than one person, and hearing a recording that the call center is "experiencing higher than normal volume" can quickly thwart the customer's expectation and desire for faster service.

Internet access (the World Wide Web) to the service provider has also helped to speed up service significantly compared to a few decades ago. The impact of internet access can be compared to telegraph and telephone systems development and proliferation. It has changed much of the way the world works and communicates. While some call centers may offer 24/7 service, virtually all service providers offer web access 24/7. When the online service provider tools work as promised, the service is experienced as fast by the customer. The customer can access the website in seconds, execute a transaction, and complete the service encounter in minutes versus the hours or days it took to conduct that same transaction just a few decades ago.

> Clearly, there is a significant overlap between service timeliness and access to the service. Access is the focus of the next chapter. However, because access and timeliness are so bound together, primarily because of enabling technology, some of the timeliness examples are also examples of access. The service provider's website is at once a tool for increased timeliness and a tool for increased access. All the elements of WACW are connected, but some are more connected than others.

As asserted several times earlier, timeliness is an expected aspect of customer service. Being on time does not typically lead to increased satisfaction, while not being timely can lead to decreased satisfaction. And in most cases, being faster than the competition may produce a short-term rise in satisfaction but will quickly become the expected. However, in some cases, timeliness may provide a long-term advantage. If a service provider can deliver information, data, or support sooner than the provider's competitors, the provider has an advantage in the marketplace—at least until the marketplace catches up. For example, in financial services, if the B2B service provider can deliver financial information (e.g., gain/loss information, balances) faster than its competitors, this may provide a significant advantage to the customer (investor).

While speed is almost always important to the customer, it becomes even more important during problem recovery. Problem recovery will be discussed in detail in a later chapter, but it is worth noting here that problem resolution will be judged in large part by how fast the provider responds to and resolves problems. It's safe to say that during problem recovery, the customer's sensitivity generally and specifically regarding timeliness is increased. A basic axiom can be used to describe waiting time during problem recovery: "Waiting during problem recovery *feels* longer than during a typical service encounter."

Just in Time (JIT)

Chapter 1 includes a brief discussion of JIT. (JIT is sometimes referred to as the Toyota Production System, named after the industry pioneer of its use.) JIT is a business process toolset that involves managing the supply chain so that manufacturing materials are on hand just before they are needed, thus reducing the cost associated with maintaining an inventory, among other benefits. While JIT is usually focused on product versus service, it's still worth including JIT in any discussion about timeliness.

With the pandemic, we've seen huge disruptions in the supply chain. JIT is a process that seems ill-equipped to respond to an unanticipated global crisis. In turn, this affects accuracy and timeliness of projections between suppliers, their business customers, and the end customer. This illustrates an unanticipated process failure, but a failure that remains unaddressed since work process is typically not designed around exceptional circumstances. However, what we've seen lately is the exceptional becoming the "new Normal," so providers may have to rethink the supply chain and JIT.

> Over the course of my career, I worked with many service provider contact centers. On many more than one occasion, a customer would complain about not receiving a call back within the time range set by the service provider. If the Customer Service Representative (CSR) was asked why they didn't make the callback, it was not uncommon to hear the CSR respond by saying they didn't have the information for the customer. Of course, the "right" answer here is to make the callback within the range, explain the situation to the customer, and reset the clock. Not doing so creates two problems: one, the customer didn't get what they wanted and, two, they didn't get a callback.

The Individual Customer's Experience of Timeliness and Managing Waiting Time

One way to define and understand the individual customer's experience of timeliness is the customer's experience of duration. How long did the customer have to wait between the point at which the service request or encounter was initiated versus the point at which the service was delivered? The customer's sense of duration is subjective. It can be influenced by an expectation set by the provider (e.g., *"Your call will be answered in 3 minutes."*). The sense of duration can also be influenced by experience with the service provider or similar providers. Perception of the urgency of the service needed can also influence the customer's experience of duration. For example, if the customer is in an emergency room waiting to be seen by a physician, the experience of duration may be a multiple of actual clock time.

For many customers, perhaps most, it feels like some service providers put up barriers to timely service delivery. Examples abound. Think of the patient in the ER waiting room who, after waiting to be seen, is taken to an exam room and then must wait some more, and then someone comes in to ask what feels like an endless stream of questions. For another example, the customer calls the service provider and gets a forced choice series of questions. And, by the way, it always seems that the provider's "menu has changed so please listen to all of the options." A third example of a perceived barrier to timely

[52]

customer service is often found when using the service provider's website. There is often too much information, poorly formatted, ineffective search functions, and too many requirements to obtain the needed service (e.g., creating an account for a one-time transaction).

Even after acknowledging the points above, technology has enabled ever-increasing timeliness or speed: better designed websites that allow users to check out as a visitor, rather than setting up a new account; and contact centers that allow callers to opt out of the initial menu by saying (or yelling) "Representative" or hitting the zero key twice. Some community health centers allow patients to self-check-in and participate in regional health information networks, so that patient information can be accessed by providers across the region, thus avoiding repetitive, time-consuming questions.

It is without question that customer waiting time in some services has decreased significantly over the past few decades. The example cited earlier of ATMs exemplifies improved timeliness via technology. ATMs can, for a simple transaction, be significantly faster than going to the bank and waiting in line to see a teller. Even at the bank, access to a teller for more complex inquiries or transactions may be timelier since the ATM is handling routine, simple transactions. Service provider websites generally have improved timeliness. State registries for motor vehicles are notorious for making the customer wait in long lines for even the most routine service. Today, the customer can update their registration *and* driver's license online, freeing up registry staff to handle more complex issues or questions.

Not surprisingly, wait time has been the subject of rigorous study with useful insights and actions that can impact the customer's perception of timeliness. David Maister, a former Harvard Business School professor, writer, and researcher, has produced an actionable list of waiting time axioms.[*] Maister's waiting time attributes are as follows: [*]

---

[*] Maister, David "The Psychology of Waiting Lines," Copyright 2005 David H. Maister

[*] Along with David Maister's principles are examples that are both original to this text or drawn from Maister's Waiting Lines article, as indicated.

1. Occupied time feels shorter than unoccupied time.

One of the clearest examples of occupying waiting time is putting a variety of magazines in the physician's waiting room. Giving restaurant patrons menus while they wait to be seated is another example. (Both of these examples are cited by Maister.) Disney theme parks are famous for their serpentine lines. At virtually every turn of the line there's a visual stimulus, movie clip, or even a Disney character to occupy customers. Maister also provides an example of playing music while a customer call is on hold. However, it should be remembered that customers did not call to hear music and that musical tastes vary widely, thus, the "wrong" music may make the wait feel longer. Regarding music while on hold, it's worth noting that when a customer calls Apple, they are given a choice about what kind of music they will hear. This occupies the customer's time as well as marketing Apple's music library.

> There is a story, perhaps apocryphal, about an elevator in a skyscraper in New York. People were complaining that the elevator took too long to get to the uppermost floors. Elevator experts and engineers were brought in. They were successful in speeding up the elevator, but the complaints continued unabated. Finally, a consultant recommended putting mirrors in the elevator. The building owner did so, and the complaints dripped off immediately. An example of occupied time.

2. People want to get started.

Customers want service to begin as soon as possible. For example, if customers calling the provider contact center were answered by a person who asked a series of qualifying questions, the customer would likely feel that their service experience began sooner than if their call was answered by a series of automated prompts—even though the total duration of the call was the same with and without the initial human contact. (Several contact centers I worked with had a standard of performance of answering calls within three rings to accelerate service delivery.)

3. Anxiety makes waiting seem longer.

Maister uses examples of waiting in line at the airport or flying standby to illustrate how anxiety makes a wait seem longer. Other examples include waiting in the doctor's office, especially after hearing about

[54]

troubling test results. Or in a situation in which the principle of occupied time feeling shorter is turned upside down. For example, the person having their teeth cleaned. For many patients, while they are certainly occupied, they are also anxious. Each minute in the dentist's chair is experienced as a multiple of itself.

4. Uncertain waits are (feel) longer than known, finite waits.

If a customer calls the service provider's contact center and is told they will have to wait on hold without also being given an expectation of how long they will have to wait, the wait will often feel longer than the actual clock time *("I was on hold forever")*. Maister gives the example of the airline pilot repeatedly telling passengers a wait will "only be for a few more minutes." In this case, the wait is both uncertain and therefore perceived as "long," as well as fostering anxiety among some passengers.

5. Unexplained waits are longer than explained waits.

If the customer is told why they must wait, they may be less dissatisfied than if no explanation is provided. For example, if a customer calling the service provider's contact center is put on hold with no explanation, not only will the experience of the waiting time feel longer than objective clock time, but it is also likely to engender dissatisfaction from "being left in the dark." By contrast, that same customer may be told, *"Are you able to hold? I need to contact our research area to look at your account history. The hold may last for several minutes/up to 5 minutes."* In this example, the customer is not "happy" to be put on hold, but they will likely feel less dissatisfied than if they were "left in the dark." Maister uses the example of an airline pilot explaining the reason for delay(s) (e.g., late baggage, weather). Again, the customer is not happy, but they are likely to be less unhappy.

6. Unfair waits are (perceived as) longer than equitable waits.

Seeing someone "jump the line" at a restaurant, grocery store, bank, etc., is likely to irritate other customers and make their wait seem longer. Even more specifically, someone at the grocery store violating the "10 items or fewer" rule in the express checkout lane will quickly earn the ire of customers following the rules and, at the same time, increase their experience of wait time. Maister uses the concept of First in First Out (FIFO) to illustrate this principle. Customers don't like it when other customers or the provider break the FIFO rule. One exception to FIFO is when the provider clearly states that some customers will be served ahead of others for a specific and valid reason (e.g., triage in a hospital emergency room).

7. The more valuable the service, the longer the customer will wait.

Maister uses the example of restaurant patrons being willing to wait for service at a 5-star restaurant versus, for example, a restaurant chain. A patient may be more willing to wait for a renowned medical specialist than a physician's assistant. Going back to a Disney theme park example, patrons may be willing to wait longer for a new or novel ride, versus waiting for a well-known amusement. The reverse of this principle is also true. Customers are unwilling to wait for less valuable service and, if forced to wait, will tend to experience the wait as longer. For example, Maister describes a customer checking out of a hotel as essentially a valueless experience and customers quickly experience time in line as onerous. That's why many hotels offer various forms of self-checkout.

8. Solo waits feel longer than group waits.

This might be characterized as the "We're all in the same boat syndrome," or even, "Misery loves company." Groups of customers who are waiting for service will tend to experience less time waiting than a customer waiting alone. Maister points out that a sense of community can develop very quickly. While he encourages providers to find ways to allow customers to experience "group waiting," another point of view is that if they do so, and collectively experience a service delay, the members of the group may feed and increase other group members' feelings of dissatisfaction.

> **Additional Note about Wait Time:** In the service operating environment, one may often hear the aphorism, "under promise and over deliver." This is often applied to timeliness. For example, telling the customer that doing something will take longer than it actually does, then delivering the service faster than expected. While this sounds good, it isn't. It's actually dangerous. The "over delivery" will become the expected delivery very quickly. Plus, if you know something can be done sooner than promised, but you under promise, you've lied to your customer—not a defensible service strategy under any circumstances.

Going back to the beginning of the discussion about timeliness, the individual customer's experience of the duration of the service encounter is almost always subjective and all too often experienced as too long. David Maister's principles about waiting time offer providers specific ideas about how to manage the experience of the customer.

Fundamentally, setting expectations for how long a wait is likely to take is something every provider can do (this echoes Maister's principle of explained waits). For example, individual customers calling the provider's contact center are frequently told to "hold on a sec," or "hold on a minute, while I look that up." The first of these commands is false. No one holds on for a "sec." The second is likely to be wrong because the wait is more or less than a minute. Instead, restating the example used earlier, the customer service representative (CSR) begins the hold by saying something like, *"Are you able to hold while I (look up your account), it may take up to 3 minutes?"* In this example the CSR is polite and specific about predicted waiting time. And the customer is given a choice.

CSRs and call center managers are likely to complain about the suggested hold protocol above. It smacks of scripting and may be awkward and time consuming to implement. Also, call center managers may not want to give the customer a choice. However, the CSR can "invest" the phrasing with a friendly tone and giving the customer a choice might be well worth it to achieve distinctive customer service (even though it may quickly become the expected level of service).

The challenge of timely service delivery to individual customers never ends. Because of improved process and technology, the "standard" for service delivery is forever a moving target. At the same time, providers must try to hit the timeliness target because not being timely, in the eyes of the individual customer, is such a powerful dissatisfier.

Normative Timeliness for B2B Customers

The B2B customer's perception of their provider's timeliness will be driven by both individual and special situations (e.g., projects, one-off requests) as well as timeliness of aggregated, routine service deliveries. Like the B2B customer's experience with accuracy, their experience of typical service timeliness will likely be norm referenced.

That is, judging a specific provider's timeliness relative to the normative timeliness of other providers delivering identical or similar services.

As noted earlier, timeliness for projects and one-off requests may be judged in the same manner that individual customers judge their service provider. Was the project completed on time, late or early? Was the special request for a report, for example, delivered in a timely manner? David Maister's principles about waiting time may not apply since institutions are not people. The psychology of an institution is different than the psychology of an individual customer. That said, some of Maister's principles may apply in some circumstances. For example, explained waits may feel shorter than unexplained waits. If the provider explains a delay to the B2B customer *before* the service is due, the customer may not feel as dissatisfied as they would with no explanation, or an explanation (or excuse) provided after the service was expected or due.

B2B customers typically have individual, or end-customers (e.g., retail customers, individual shareholders, healthcare patients).These end-customers are often serviced by the B2B service provider. Like accuracy, the end-customer can be a "wild-card" that disrupts the concept of norm referenced timeliness. For example, a specific end-customer might be defined as uniquely important (e.g., family of the provider's board of directors, a high dollar customer, an internet influencer). If the uniquely important end-customer experiences a timeliness problem, it may become disproportionally important to the institutional customer. Thus, even though the overall timeliness rate is at or better than the norm, a complaint from a uniquely important customer can force the service provider to respond disproportionally, inefficiently expending time and resources around a single issue, representing the smallest fraction of total service interactions.

Timeliness In Relation to the Other Elements of What All Customers Want (WACW)

Timeliness and Accuracy: This relationship was described in the previous chapter focused on accuracy, but it is worth reviewing here. Accurate information, data or assistance that is delivered late may or may not be judged as accurate. It might be accurate if the information or data is stable and unchanging from when it was requested to the point at which it was delivered, even if it's late. However, as asserted in the accuracy discussion, if the information, data, or assistance must be delivered on time to be judged as accurate, then late delivery must be judged as not only late, but also as inaccurate. As stated in the previous chapter, if the customer wants to purchase company stock at a specific price and is given old or late (stale) pricing information, the price given to the customer can be judged as not only late, but also incorrect. The customer's decisions based on late information/data will be flawed.

Timeliness and Access: No connection between the components of WACW is stronger than that between timeliness and access. Service providers who provide online access to conduct transactions, telephone contact centers, and stand-alone technology like ATMs, among other service channels, are simultaneously providing their customers with increased access and increased timeliness precisely because of that access. For example, especially during the pandemic, a regional or local bank customer need never physically enter the bank's property for months or even years. Deposits, transfers, and withdrawals can be accomplished via computer or handheld device. For some banks and some customers, even more complex transactions such as lines of credit or equity loans can be established online. Thinking back just a couple of decades, accessing the bank transactions cited above would have taken hours, days, or even weeks.

Timeliness and Usefulness: In at least some cases, if the service delivery is late, it makes the service (e.g., information, data) less useful or even useless. For example, if cost/price or return on investment data is delivered late, the use of such data is at least diminished and perhaps even dangerous, in that it might mislead the customer and result in a poor decision. Likewise, being early in delivering service may make that delivery less useful or even useless. The same example from above applies here. Specifically, changing price or cost data the delivery of which must be on time to be useful—not late, not early. It should also be understood that early, faster than expected service delivery also quickly becomes the expected level of performance.

Timeliness and Responsiveness: For many, perhaps most customers, being timely is a big part of being responsive. If the customer must wait beyond the expected amount of time on the phone or online for the service delivery, that service may be judged as unresponsive, even when the online service delivery is successful, and the CSR demonstrates an array of effective behaviors. Compounding customer dissatisfaction with timeliness, all too often, the service provider's representative may demonstrate poor behavior. For example, (this has happened to me many times) the customer is physically waiting in line for a service (e.g., checking into a hotel) and the person responsible for service takes a phone call without acknowledging the customer in front of them. Even worse, but not uncommon, the service person takes the call, doesn't make any eye contact with the physical customer, and holds up their finger at the customer in line. This is late and unresponsive, even rude. The foregoing example can be reversed to deliver timely and responsive customer service. In this case, the hotel employee can manage the waiting time of both the customer in line and on the phone. Without going into too much detail here, the service representative can use tone, gestures, facial expression to manage the service delivery. (Much more on this later in the chapter focused on responsiveness.)

Timeliness and Problem Recovery: Two points can be made here concerning the relationship between timeliness and problem recovery. The first is that a timeliness problem is *always* present when there is another service problem. For example, the customer comes in, calls in, or goes online for service. The service delivered is inaccurate, inaccessible, not useful, or delivered by an unresponsive service representative. The customers didn't get what they wanted *when* they wanted it. Thus, there is a timeliness problem along with any other problem. The second point that can be made, as was made earlier during problem recovery, the customer's sensitivity generally and specifically regarding timeliness is increased—*waiting during problem recovery feels longer than during a typical service encounter.* The service provider that invests in problem recovery process and methods will always get a solid return on the investment.

Some Examples of Timeliness for Certain Types of Customers

The following table does *not* present an exhaustive list of all customer types, service providers, or types of timeliness important to the customer. These examples illustrate the diversity of customers and the types of timeliness they might expect.

Customer Type	Provider Type	Timeliness Type
Individual Customers (in general)	Service Providers	• Precision timeliness if a precise expectation has been set (e.g., "You'll receive a callback at 4:00 p.m. EST) • Timely enough to meet the customer's request/expressed need (e.g., I need [it] by Monday, July 2nd)
Financial Service End Customer	Financial Service Provider (e.g., Banks, Investment Firms)	• Precision timeliness • Timely enough based on the expectation set (see examples above)
Employee (all levels, all types)	Employee's Supervisor/Manager	Fast—delivery of feedback about a specific incident is within hours of the incident
Employee (all levels, all types)	The Provider Company/ Corporation	Timeliness of compensation increases and/or bonus compares favorably to the norm for the same job in the same region
Client Facing Employees (e.g., CSRs)	End Customers	Precision timeliness regarding the information/data needed from the customer to provide service (e.g., exact dates, times)
Supervisor/ Manager	Employees	• Precision timeliness from employees who must be available to begin working at a specific time (e.g., call center reps at their desk, ready to take calls at a precise time) • Timely enough (within a range of a few minutes) for back-office employees
Institutional Customer	Institutional Provider	Norm-Referenced Timeliness

Continued →

Customer Type	Provider Type	Timeliness Type
Healthcare Patient	Healthcare Provider	• Precision timeliness for medication regimen • Timely enough for test results • Fast for test results concerning a serious condition
Healthcare Provider	Patient	Timely enough input from the patient about their experience and behavior (e.g., symptoms, habits, diet, and exercise) **Note:** The experienced provider may be able to account for exaggeration and omission.
Employee's Colleagues	Employee	General adherence to company rules/expectations about timeliness expectations (e.g., arrival time, breaks, quitting time)
Community Member	Local Government	Norm-referenced timeliness regarding community services provided
Local Government	Community Member	Norm-referenced timeliness with regard to use of community services
Students	Teachers	• Timely enough teaching delivery • Fast feedback regarding specific performance (e.g., very positive, very negative, critical to student progress)
Teachers	Students	Precision timeliness when a precise expectation is set (e.g., papers are due via email no later than 12:01 on September 23)

A Call to Action

As stated previously, the best way to understand the elements of WACW is to apply it to real world circumstances. Thus, to fully understand timeliness, you can define how it applies to one or more of your customers. For example, if you are a manager of multiple teams employing multiple team members, each under the direction of one or more front-line supervisors, those supervisors are your customers. Each can feel satisfied or dissatisfied about what you do, and they can act individually or collectively based on their satisfaction or dissatisfaction.

Ask yourself, what do the front-line supervisors under your management expect/want from you in relation to timeliness? An example follows, but your own application to your own situation will be much more meaningful and useful.

Your Supervisors want...	Specific Example(s)
Precision Timeliness	You provide precise expectations for when routine and non-routine work output from the supervisor's team must be completed. For example: • Team staffing report is due at 4:00 p.m. every other Friday (early or late reporting will not be accurate/useful) • For the team working with customers over the phone, average "talk-time" does not exceed 2 minutes, 30 seconds
Individual Supervisor's Waiting Time	For any delays in your managerial functions involving individual supervisors (e.g., staff meetings, one-on-one feedback) an explanation for the delay is provided (an application of David Maister's waiting time axioms).
Timely Enough	You set aside every Wednesday afternoon from 1:00 p.m. to 4:00 p.m. as office hours for ad hoc supervisor meetings, questions, or assistance.
Fast or Faster	You are available to supervisors within 60 minutes of a request for assistance in handling an exception or problem. A specific alternate is assigned and identified if you will not be available.

Going through this process for yourself in relation to one or more of your internal or external customers is an effort that will solidify your understanding of timeliness as part of WACW. Your initial effort may be imperfect, but over time, it will become increasingly accurate and useful.

A few final points about timeliness:

1. Remember that the customer's experience of the passage of time is often entirely subjective. Thus, you may want to synchronize your watch with the customer. This advisory can be taken literally. For example, you're on the phone with your customer and you need to call them back after doing some research. You might say, "It's 9:15 a.m. EST my time. I'll call you back between 2:00 and 2:15 p.m. EST. At that point, I will either have the information you need, or I'll give you a progress report and set a new time for completion."

2. Some timeliness expectations (standards) can be set for the long-term and only revisited periodically. For example, setting a precise timeliness expectation for when a call center or service center lobby will be open and closed. Other timeliness expectations are situational. The example given in number one above applies to a specific situation.

3. It would be wrong to generalize the timeliness expectations of different generations (e.g., Baby Boomers versus Millennials). However, it is interesting and perhaps worthwhile to think about what the different generations are used to, or expect, from their service provider relative to timeliness. It's fair to say that generation Z (millennials 1997—2021) have typically received faster service across their lives than Baby Boomers (1946—1964). It may also be fair to say that each succeeding generation receives faster service, often via technology, than the preceding generation, and that timeliness expectations contract as the years pass and that what satisfied one generation won't satisfy the next. My kids expect things to happen faster than I do and while I might be satisfied with a certain timeliness performance, my kids would be dissatisfied. Providers who understand the demographic of their customers would do well to understand the generational forces at work governing the perception of timeliness.

Next, Access will be discussed as an integral component of WACW.

The internet gave us access to everything; but
it also gave everything access to us.

—James Veitech

I do not fear computers. I fear the lack of them.

—Isaac Asimov

The internet is a telephone that's gotten uppity.

—Clifford Stoll

Chapter 4

Access

*A customer is anyone in a position to feel satisfied or dissatisfied about **access** and can act based on their satisfaction or dissatisfaction.*

At first glance, access as part of What All Customers Want (WACW), seems less important than accuracy and timeliness. After all, accuracy and timeliness are foundational, while access isn't something most people think about in the same way. However, if the service provider is accurate and timely but the customer can't access the service, accuracy and timeliness don't matter—they can't be accessed. Likewise, the same is true for the other elements of WACW, namely, utility, responsiveness, and problem recovery. Access has a make-or-break impact on these elements in the same way being inaccessible impacts accuracy and timeliness. If the customer can't access the service, the other elements of the WACW don't matter. Thus, like all of the components of WACA, access becomes hierarchically most important when there is a problem.

More specific than the touchstone definition that starts this chapter, access is defined here as *the ability of the customer to get at the service they want, when they want, using the means they want.* From this definition and from the discussion in the previous chapter on timeliness, it is readily apparent that timeliness and access have a strong connection. A new means of access is often developed precisely because it makes access to the service faster.

The second part of the definition, access *using the means the customer wants*, is a little less clear than the connection between access—when the customer wants to access the service—and timeliness. For example, the customer may want access to a person in a telephone contact center, but the provider's primary means of access, especially after hours, is through the provider's website. The customer is still offered access, but not the way some customers want. Thus, the customer may be a little irritated, dissatisfied, or very dissatisfied (the latter result being more likely if the customer doesn't have internet access, has a physical challenge that makes using a computer difficult, or a strong antipathy toward computers in general). In contrast, some customers prefer internet access to a provider website and speaking with a telephone representative is the last thing they want. For these customers, having to speak with a service person is experienced as limiting access. Limits on access may affect some customers but not others, but it's still a limit. Most service providers are on a constant quest to improve and increase access and the quest must be constant since the service provider's competitors are continuously doing the same thing.

In the chapters covering accuracy and timeliness, it was asserted that they are most often expected from the provider and become strong dissatisfiers if service is not accurate or not timely. Access is similar in some ways and different in others. Access is similar to accuracy and timeliness since once access is provided, it becomes expected; the failure of access, or as described above, limited access, will often drive dissatisfaction. Access is different because a new and effective means of access may drive satisfaction up for a considerable period and, in some cases, become a relatively long-term differentiator (satisfier) between service providers.

Like accuracy and timeliness, there are several ways to define and describe access:

- Physical, Face-to-Face Access to Service
- Telephone Access
- Access via Specialized Technology
- Access via the Internet
- Access by B2B Customers

Physical, Face-to-Face Access to Service

This form of access to service extends back millennia, through the present day, and presumably into the future, for as long as there are service providers and customers. Face-to-face service delivery is the chosen mode of receiving service for some customers, and it may be the preferred mode of access if a service problem occurs. The flip side of this preference is also present and growing. Some customers prefer access via technology, even when face-to-face service is available.

It is self-evident that customer service, once the exclusive realm of the face-to-face service provider/representative, has been significantly altered because of technology. Initially, the change in access was exemplified by telephone service, then by large volume telephone contact centers, and presently by specialized service kiosks and, more generally, by internet access. However, it is important to stipulate that face-to-face service has not, and probably will not, ever be absent as a form of customer service delivery, even when it is provided in tandem with technology-based access. Some examples of face-to-face service at present that will probably extend into the indefinite future—again, in tandem with other access channels—are:

- Healthcare professionals and especially medical specialists (even with the advent of telemedicine)
- Lawyers and accountants
- Bank service representatives (e.g., tellers, loan officers, notary public personnel)
- Concierge service provided on a limited basis to certain qualified customers (e.g., airline clubs, special floors in a hotel).
- Flight attendants and ticket agents
- Front-line service personnel of large and small retail stores/ outlets (in which compensation is not commission based)
- Restaurant workers (front of house)
- Grocery store workers
- Priority service providers serving high value customers and/or engaged in problem recovery
- Teachers
- Wealth management professionals
- (Internal customers) employees, colleagues, support personnel, supervisors, managers, etc.

> We have all had experience with the preference of one type of access over another. I remember being at my bank and seeing people queue up for the ATM even though there was no line to access a teller. It can be argued that for a routine transaction, such as a balance inquiry or withdrawal, electronic access may be preferred because it's experienced as faster and more dependable than a live teller. Further, the bank customer may simply prefer not to interact with a person. However, as stated a few times elsewhere, if a service problem occurs, that same customer may prefer face-to-face service access.

Customers will judge the quality of their access in a face-to-face service encounter in several ways:

- How quickly was the customer able to access a person who could help them (this goes back to timeliness, discussed in the previous chapter)?

- Was the face-to-face service representative able to provide the service sought?

- Was the behavior of the service representative polite and professional (this includes tone and facial expression)?

- Did the service representative listen (the upcoming chapter on Responsiveness will go into detail about listening as a foundational service behavior)?

- How long did the face-to-face service encounter take, from inception to completion?

- Did the customer leave the service interaction feeling confident that the "right" service was provided (e.g., correct, relevant, complete)?

It's worth noting that the front-line face-to-face service employee is often paid less than the U.S. average for wage earners—$31,083 versus $51,916.* Front-line service workers are often entry-level positions and in large organizations, may be working in a team of 15 to 20 people. These are the same people providing face-to-face service to customers who will feel satisfied or dissatisfied with their service experience and may act based on their satisfaction or dissatisfaction (e.g., positive/negative reviews, telling others).

It is important for the service provider organization to understand that for the customer, the service person they interact with face-to-face *is* the provider organization. (This may be especially true for employees—as customers—having a face-to-face interaction with their supervisor or manager.) Thus, it makes sense for the provider organization to ensure front-line, client facing personnel are compensated fairly for the work and the region (a regional, norm-referenced total compensation package), that they receive training

---

* Based on a quick Google search of average salaries for front-line service personnel versus the average for U.S. wage earners in general.

commensurate with their job, that the work environment actively excludes bias (e.g., race, gender), that they receive feedback from a credible source and access to development opportunities, and that they have access to career growth commensurate with their performance and qualifications.

Telephone Access

While the first telephones were developed in the late 19th century, they didn't come into wide-spread consumer use until the early 20th century. By 1903, there were over 2 million telephones. By 1938 there were 30 million, and in 2020 there were over 284 million smart-phones in the U.S. alone. The first use of a national number plan (AKA area codes) didn't happen until 1946. From the end of WWII forward, through the next two decades or so, the phone increasingly became part of the landscape, at home, at work, in public buildings, and on the streets. In the early days (both before and after the war), a person didn't just pick up the phone and make a call, they had to go through an operator, *which may be the earliest example of telephone-based customer service.*

In the 1960s through the early 2000s, large banks of public phones could be found in every airport, train station, hotel, and public building. Fast forward to the second decade of the 21st century, and it's almost impossible to find a phone booth anywhere. Portable phones came into being in the early '70s.

While they are still called phones, they are now often referred to as handheld devices or smart phones, since they do much more than a phone. In the 2020s, handheld devices are everywhere in the developed world.

Phones profoundly changed the way service is delivered to customers. It's hard to put an exact date on it, but certainly through the early 1960s, customer service was delivered almost exclusively through face-to-face contact with the service provider. The postal service was also a channel for accessing service, albeit very (very) slowly by today's standards. For some customers and some service providers, telephone access began early in the 20th century and continues through the present day. A customer can access their lawyer, accountant, or doctor, among other providers, via the phone. However, it is less likely that the actual service delivery will be completed over the phone. It is

[71]

more likely that the initial phone access will be a precursor to a face-to-face appointment, or a later and more substantive call. What's different now versus a decade or two ago is what, for example, a patient hears when accessing their doctor over the phone. The patient will hear a menu of options. Thus, even though the patient's call was answered in just a few rings, they may not have accessed the service needed—unless the call was to get hours of operation, an address, or other static information. Access, as it is defined in relation to WACW, means the customer, in this example a patient, *"gets what they want, when they want it."* Some customers may experience the ubiquitous use of menu prompts as providing less access than years ago, when the call was typically answered by a person.

> **A personal example:** When I call my doctor, on every call I hear the address and phone number of the office. More recently, this information is preceded by a COVID-related announcement. The total time for these messages is almost a full minute before I get to the menu of prompts. At the same time, it is reasonable to infer that most callers are repeat callers—as I am. Thus, I have no need or interest in the repetition of the same information every time I call. This is not access, this is not timely, let alone "fast" as discussed in the preceding chapter. What's the answer? Make the static information available toward the end of the menu prompts, after offering an appointment and prescription refill options—arguably the most frequent reasons for a patient call. (It must be acknowledged that there may be legal/liability concerns relative to the placement of the COVID announcement.)

The 1-800 service began in the late sixties and with it, the first call centers were created. A call center employs Customer Service Representatives (CSRs) to answer customer calls and provide service. Presently, it is hard to find a large service organization that does not provide access via a call center (often called contact centers). Financial service firms, insurance providers, airlines, various government departments/agencies, hotels, and car rental providers, are among some of the large organizations using call centers.

Today, call centers are the norm. The call center may be owned and operated by the service provider company, or they may be "white label" providers; organizations providing call center outsource capabilities to a specific marketplace as their core business. Also, call centers may be onshore, near shore, or offshore.

On paper at least, service provider call centers offer almost ideal access. The customer simply calls the provider's call center, either in-house or white label (outsourced), makes the service request, which is fulfilled quickly and accurately, and the entire service experience satisfies the customer. However, since we've all had problems accessing our service providers (e.g., long waits/holds, getting passed around the center, long initial menu prompts), it would be easy to be cynical or sarcastic about accessing providers via a call center. Nevertheless, the reality is that there are millions of customer-initiated service calls every day and most of them provide reasonably good (not dissatisfying) access.

Access problems when a customer calls for service tend to fall into one or more of the following types:

- Excessive waits until the call is answered. Twenty to thirty seconds of Average Wait Time (AWT) is an accepted standard. Making the customer wait beyond or well beyond the AWT can be defined as excessive.

- Hearing the recorded message, *"We are experiencing higher than average call volumes, so waiting time may be longer than normal."* (Some providers are starting to provide an estimated wait time. This conforms with David Maister's axiom about explained or predicable waits feeling shorter than unexplained or unpredictable waits, but there is still an access problem.)

- Hearing the message, *"Our menu has changed recently,"* is an access problem because it forces the caller to wait and wade through, potentially, the entire menu. (And it seems that every provider's menu has changed recently.)

- Menu prompts that don't begin with the most frequent service request; for example, the pharmacy chain that puts prescription refills as the third or fourth choice on the menu. An example used earlier is illustrative of this access problem; when the recorded message begins with a generic announcement (about COVID, for example) and then static information (e.g., hours of operation, the street address).

- Getting through to a CSR only to be put on hold for an excessive amount of time—more than 2 to 3 minutes. This access problem becomes even more dissatisfying when no hold time estimate is provided by the CSR, or having waited, the customer request cannot be fulfilled.

- Related to the preceding point, the customer is told they must call another number (instead of a "warm" transfer to that number, conducted by the initial CSR).

- Getting through to a CSR who is hard to hear, speaks too quickly, has a strong accent, or uses unusual word order (e.g., referring to the customer as "Mr. John" versus "Mr. Jones).

- Not being given a way to quickly get out of the menu and speak with a live CSR. Some providers provide a way to get out of the menu by pressing "0" twice; others ask the customer to say "Representative."

The list of call center access problems above is representative, not exhaustive. Also, some of the access problems could also be defined as timeliness or responsiveness problems. This is intentional and necessary since all the elements of WACW overlap one another.

An additional note about call center access: customers can buy increased, better access. For example, most credit card companies offer premium cards and premium access. The customer is given a "special" number, the call will likely be answered by a person and that person has more authority than the typical contact center CSR. Obviously, the premium service comes at a premium price—a multiple of the annual fee for the basic, no frills credit card.

How can call centers improve the customers' experience of access?

- Use up-to-date, reliable telephone call center technology for handling inbound and outbound calls (e.g., Computer/Telephone Integration, Automatic Call Distributor, Call Recording Systems, Noise Canceling Systems). Notice this is not a recommendation for "bleeding-edge" technology. Systems reliability is paramount for call centers.

- Effectively manage the Automatic Call Distributor (ACD system). The ACD can be compared to an air traffic control system in that it requires a high level of skills to use and manage effectively.

- Have and maintain the right staffing levels to achieve the 2 to 3 minutes of average wait time. The provider, whether in-house

[74]

or outsourced, cannot be expected to staff based on exceptional circumstances, but many times, these circumstances
can be predicted in a way that allows for increased staffing
(e.g., a persistent trend in the stock market—up or down).

- Manage your menu. Keep it as simple as possible. Change it
  very seldom. Put frequent service types up front. Give your
  customers a way out.

- Remember, hearing music is not access. But, as an aside, Apple
  gives customers a choice of what type of music they hear while
  waiting or on hold (conforming with Maister's "occupied time"
  axiom).

- Deliver on the "one stop shopping" principle. This means equipping CSRs with the right skills, knowledge, authority, and technology to handle almost any customer request. In the event a
  transfer is needed, ensure that the initial CSR stays with the
  customer until the "expert" is on the line.

- Train your CSRs to speak at a moderate pace, use proper dic-
  tion, avoid colloquialisms, and diminish strong accents. (This
  topic will be addressed in greater detail in the chapter on
  Responsiveness.)

A Note about Technology Problem Prevention and Resilience

Problem prevention means designing systems that can resist both naturally-occurring service interruptions (e.g., weather-related power outages) and malicious attacks (e.g., viruses, malware). Resilience means effectively recovering from a problem and returning to, in the case of technology, an operable state. Telephone and computer technology that provide access to service by customers must be both resistant to malicious or natural threats and resilient when such threats are realized. Prevention and resilience have become increasingly important over the past couple of decades and are presently an integral part of the design, implementation, and ongoing operation of customer service technologies. The pandemic, global warming as a catalyst for extreme weather, and the vulnerability of the power grid to both natural and man-made disasters among other threats will continue to make problem prevention (e.g., systems hardening) and resilience a top priority for service providers offering technology-based access to service.

As a final note on telephone access, it is important to reiterate that a customer is *anyone* able to feel satisfied with what you/the service provider does and can act based on their satisfaction or dissatisfaction. Thus, the front-line employee is the customer of their supervisor, the supervisor is a customer of the front-line employee, and so on throughout the organization. As we continue to move forward into the second decade of the 21st century, work-at-home is no longer the exception. It's become commonplace. As a result, the phone has become one of the main channels for accessing collegial support, employee direction and feedback, supervisory support, and a host of other internal support services (e.g., Human Resources, technology support, product support). The best practices for external customer phone access to their provider (some of which are cited earlier) readily apply to the internal customer dynamic (e.g., employees should be able to quickly phone their supervisor for advice/direction).

Access via Specialized Technology

Specialized technology is technology that gives the customer access via self-service. Using this technology, the customer can quickly access and acquire what they want, when they want it. Self-service technology eliminates the human service representative, providing contactless and frictionless service, *until something goes wrong*. Access via specialized technology can produce a rise in customer satisfaction when it's new to customers, easy to use, automates previously time-consuming access methods, and is reliable. As time passes, the self-service technology becomes an expected customer service, no longer raising customer satisfaction, and producing potentially high levels of dissatisfaction when the technology is inaccessible (e.g., fails to work as promised, offline, down for service, not in a convenient location). For service providers, self-service technology provides significant long-term gains and benefits (e.g., service delivery cost savings, freeing up employees for more complex tasks.) For front-line service delivery personnel, the dark-side of self-service technology is, potentially at least, lay-offs and, generally, a reduced need for certain types of employees.

ATMs are a prime example of self-service technology and have been extensively used in this and preceding chapters as a customer service tool for accuracy, timeliness, and access. The customer doesn't need to interact with a service person and can achieve their service goal independent of any outside intervention. All the customer needs for 24/7 access to an ATM is to be a bank customer with an ATM card and have a unique 4- or 5-digit access code. While ATMs began as simple cash dispensers, nowadays, beyond simple transactions such as accessing account balances and making cash withdrawals, many contemporary ATMs offer a range of services, including deposits, transfers, or even applying for loan.

> ATMs are ubiquitous. They can engender a satisfied customer, particularly when features are added that are of value to bank customers. For example, some banks offer no fee withdrawals from ATMs fielded by other banks, giving the customer a clear reward and the provider a competitive advantage. Simply having more ATMs than a local competitor may also have a positive customer impact. Going back to the beginning of ATM technology in the 1960s and 70s, a piece of advertising illustrates the power of access. According to an article in Wikipedia, in 1969, Chemical Bank, an early adopter of ATMs, used the tag line, *"On Sept. 2 our bank will open at 9:00 and never close."* (It should be noted that ATM growth is declining with the advent of cashless payment systems like Apple Pay and PayPal and, at some future point, may be replaced altogether by a myriad of other access technologies. More on this later.)

It is interesting to note that some ATMs are owned and operated by banks, while others are owned and operated by a third party offering white-label ATMs to multiple service providers. This can become an access issue if the ATM doesn't work. If the non-functional ATM is co-located with a bank lobby, the customer may go to a teller to conduct the transaction. Thus, access is provided but delayed. If the ATM isn't co-located with the bank, access is denied. In both cases, if the customer complains or simply asks when the ATM will return to service, if it is owned by a third party, the bank service person may not have an answer. This may frustrate and further dissatisfy the already dissatisfied customer.

Self-service, single, or narrow function ticketing kiosks, almost as widespread as ATMs, are a central means for service access. Ticketing kiosk examples include transportation ticketing (e.g., air and train), car parking lots, hotel check in/out, and entertainment access (e.g., movies, sporting events, concerts). Like ATMs, when kiosks first come on the scene, customer satisfaction may rise, but they soon become an expected avenue for service. Self-service checkout at grocery stores, pharmacies, and other product/service settings is yet another example of specialized technology aimed at increased access to service and lower costs for the service provider. Self-checkout technology shifts work from a service provider employee to the customer. Self-service checkout technology is not without controversy. Some research suggests that most consumers think self-service checkout is faster than waiting in line, but some consumers worry about the cleanliness/hygiene of the self-checkout area. More than two thirds of consumers responding to a survey (by Raydiant) said they had experienced a failure of the self-service checkout technology.[*]

> **Personal anecdote:** My wife and I use a grocery store and pharmacy that offers self-service checkout. Our experience has largely been negative, especially when purchasing produce, where you must look up the item versus scanning a bar code. The systems in both stores seem to fail more often than function properly. The system does not provide better access. The experience is very dissatisfying. This being said, I have a friend who feels exactly the opposite, preferring self-service checkout.

What can service providers do to deliver effective access via specialized technology? First and foremost, providers need to look at how and when customers use self-technology and then develop and update the technological access channels in a way that reflects the customer's needs and desires. Among some best practices are:

- Keep it simple, ensuring the fewest possible "clicks" to get to what the customer wants. A negative example provides an illustration. Some ATMs force the customer to pick currency denominations before dispensing the cash. For most customers, this is a meaningless and time-consuming step in the withdrawal process.

- Locate and expand access to self-service technology to places most convenient for the customer.

- Since non-functioning self-service technology can be so dissatisfying, make access to repair and servicing a top priority.

[*] "67% of consumers have had a self-service checkout fail—report," March 10, 2021, Tatiana Walk-Morris, © 2022 Industry Dive (Reporting on research from Raydiant)

- Along with the point above, it is a well-known phenomenon that new technology is often plagued by bugs, undiscovered until deployment. Thus, while new providers need to be aware of new technologies, they may be well served to stay slightly behind the curve than on the cutting edge of new technology deployment.

- Ensure that functionality of self-service technology compares favorably with norms in the marketplace.

- Notwithstanding the two previous points, if the provider does move into the delivery of new functionality to obtain a competitive advantage, do so on a limited basis initially to test both the new functionality and customer desire/satisfaction.

> **A note about email:** Many, perhaps most, websites offer an email contact if the customer wants it. This is usually a static element on the website, independent of the particular "page" customer is on. While email can be an effective means of access, new technologies such as texting and live chat may, along with other new technologies, eclipse email as a preferred means of access. At some point, it is not inconceivable that email access will be viewed similarly to letter writing and sending via the postal service. At present though, email is a significant access channel, especially, as will be discussed next, for the B2B customer.

Access via the Internet

As asserted earlier, the rapid growth and accessibility of the internet can be compared with the advent and growth of historical technology innovations (e.g., telegraph, telephone, radio, television). It's not hyperbole to say that broad based access to the internet, at least in most of the developed world, has changed almost everything. It has certainly changed how customers interact with their service providers. Nowadays, customers can use their computers, tablets, and smart phones to access their various service providers very quickly.

The history of the internet isn't widely understood and is probably of little interest to the typical customer. However, the history of the internet is also a history of ever-increasing timeliness, accuracy, and usefulness. Perhaps not surprisingly, the internet finds its beginning in the 1960s at MIT with a collaboration between an MIT professor (J.C.R. Licklider) with the U.S. Department of Defense Advanced

Research Projects Agency (DARPA). Work by other scientists led, in 1969, to a plan for the creation of ARPANET (Advanced Research Projects Agency), the first iteration of today's internet. In the early days, computer networks came into being, allowing for information sharing and collaborative work by those on the network. In the 1970s, USENET (User Network) was developed, linking networks over phone lines (remember modems?). The first commercial network, Telenet, comes in the early 1980s. What we now know of as the World Wide Web comes in the 1990s and along with it comes early websites, objectionable content, music and video pirating, and the broad concept of Cyberspace. The 2000s sees the growth and crash of the dotcom bubble, Google's and Amazon's rapid growth, the early iteration and growth of WIFI, and the advent of the so called Dark Web. As we proceed further into the 21st century, the internet is threaded into the everyday lives of almost everyone in the developed world, bringing with it advances in timeliness, access, usefulness, and the other elements of WACW to a level undreamed of just a few decades ago.

Among all its other uses, the internet has become a main channel for requesting and receiving customer service. Service providers, from the very small to the very large, have websites accessible by their customers. Typically, the websites offer access to both information and transactional services. While some websites represent a single service provider, others represent a host of providers (e.g., a patient information and a transactional portal representing a network of healthcare providers—for making appointments, obtaining test results, and messaging providers). In the present day, websites can be developed at relatively low cost and are very easy to develop. So much so that individuals offering narrow, very specialized services, or access to products can build and deploy their own website, although many individuals will opt for Facebook (Meta), TikTok, LinkedIn, or similar outlets for creating an online presence.

In the early days—the 90s and early 2000s—provider websites were typically accessed via computer using a modem and later WIFI. Presently, smartphones and tablets can be used to access service providers. Recognizing that customers will increasingly use alternatives to laptops and desktops, many providers (especially the large ones) have designed their websites to accommodate handheld devices. According to a report posted by CNBC based on research from the World

Advertising Research Center, almost three quarters of internet users will access the web via their smartphones by 2025. It's worth speculating that other technologies may emerge toward widespread use in upcoming years (e.g., smart glasses, smart contact lenses). It is possible that these new technologies will replace or offset handheld devices for web access to provider services.

Even a limited search yields some common attributes of an effective service provider website. The following is representative of website best practices:

- Simple, consistent, and attractive is better than complex and crowded. It is always tempting for the provider to overload the customer with content and options, and "attractive" is in the eye of the beholder. Web design has become a profession and it's best to use a professional *with a proven track record.* (Providers *must* check references.)

- As described earlier, handheld mobile devices are increasingly the customer's chosen vehicle for accessing the web. Thus, websites should be designed with the mobile device user in mind. This emphasizes the preceding point about simplicity of design.

- Easy, intuitive navigation of the website is a predictor of its success with customers. Ideally, the customer should be no more than two to three clicks away from successfully completing a transaction (e.g., obtaining the information sought, making an appointment, ordering goods or services).

- Effective search engine functionality is one of the keys to an effective provider website. This means making the search engine itself easily located (e.g., top right of page). Also, ensure that what the customer sees after hitting *enter* to search, contains the search word or phrase, hierarchically ranked, in the list of results.

- Effective websites include what is called in the literature and on the web, a Call to Action (CTAs). CTAs are used to encourage customer action (e.g., subscribe to service, make an appointment). Effective CTAs make clear precisely what is being offered to the customer. Like the point made earlier, providers should be using an expert in web design; an expert with successful CTA experience.

[81]

- The best websites are fast. In fact, search engines like Google consider site speed in search ranking (e.g., load speed, navigation speed). (This is another example of the special relationship of timeliness and access in WACW.)

- Most websites offer email, live chat, instant messaging, and/or a telephone contact center number.

- Make the website access for customers with disabilities or special needs. This can mean enabling voice navigation, using audible prompts, high contrast color usage, and keyboard versus mouse navigation. It may be in the provider and customer's best interest to have separate, easy to access websites for special needs users.

One way to identify typical problems with website access is to simply flip over the best practices (e.g., site not designed for mobile users, no clear CTA, not accessible to special needs customers). Some other problems, even if they are addressed in the best practices, are worth restating and other, additive problems, can be identified.

- **Passwords:** Even though most computers and handheld devices capture and auto populate passwords, they can still be problematic, even infuriating. If the consumer changes the device used to access websites, or there is a systems upgrade, or suddenly the customer's passwords simply don't work, or any number of other password problems customers experience with the provider go from being positive or unbiased to being extremely dissatisfying. Passwords and two-factor authorization are necessary but will hopefully be replaced by biometrics in the next several years (e.g., increased facial recognition, retinal scanning).

- **Slow access:** Slow load times, slow navigation, slow responses are all frustrating to very frustrating for customers. Interestingly, what may be judged as slow in the present day might have been judged as lightning fast just a few years ago (e.g., using a banking website today versus having to go to the bank a few years ago, or access via modem). The customer's perception of the speed of access is often norm-referenced. So, for example, if the customer can go onto Google and get what they want in a few seconds, then another provider's website may feel slow in comparison.

- **Outdated websites:** Especially for small service providers, there may be a temptation to have their website built, launched, and then left alone for months and even years. The website was cutting edge in 2014, but within just a few years or even less, the website is archaic. To remain effective, a website should be subject to regular analysis (at least twice a year or more often) of functionality, traffic, ease of navigation looks and feel, usefulness of the search engine, etc.

If there is a single effective prescription for building and maintaining effective website design and deployment, it is to hire an expert for initial and ongoing development. An expert is not an IT person or a graphic designer. A website expert brings together multiple disciplines and experience. Most important for selecting an expert, whether as an employee or a contractor, is their track-record. *Past performance is the best predictor of future performance.*

Access by B2B Customers

Most of the preceding information and ideas about access focus on the individual end-customer, with a few references to the service provider's internal customers. B2B customers—a business being served by another business—are different. B2B customers can access their B2B service provider by all the preceding access channels (i.e., face-to-face, phones, specialized technology, and internet) and a few more. B2B customers make extensive use of email and one-on-one phone calls, especially if the customer has a dedicated service team and a Client Relationship Manager (CRM). Video calls are also used by B2B customers, either via commercially available tools (e.g., Zoom), or in the case of large providers, in-house video conferencing technology.

As stated for other elements of WACW, the B2B customer's satisfaction with provider access may be norm-referenced. Access to one provider is assessed by comparing the experience of access to other providers in the broad business-to-business marketplace. As a result, it is possible for the service provider to distinguish itself positively or negatively by offering better or poorer access than other providers. Of note is the callback and email responsiveness. A B2B customer may call or email an individual in the service provider organization (e.g., the CRM). The speed of the callback or email, along with the quality of response, may be a key factor in judging access to the provider. (This may also be true for end-customers, but they may only be looking for a response in limited circumstances, whereas the B2B customer may routinely reach out to their provider. Again, especially if they have a dedicated service team and/or a CRM.)

Access in Relation to the Other Elements of What All Customers Want (WACW)

Access and Accuracy

No matter how fast and easy it is to access, inaccurate or incomplete information or data produces a negative customer experience. Likewise, accurate and complete information that is inaccessible or hard to access is also unacceptable to the customer. In fact, incorrect, incomplete, or inaccessible information or data can all be defined as inaccessible, since it isn't what the customer wanted from the service. The ideal state is one in which the information or data is correct (perhaps even *precisely* correct) and easily accessed via the "channel" chosen by the customer (e.g., a phone call, the provider's website).

Access and Timeliness

As described a few times earlier, timeliness and access enjoy a special connection as elements of WACW. While all the elements of WACW are connected, timeliness is often defined as an integral part of access. The customer *wants access **when** they want it.* This often means immediately, fast, or faster. The customer's expectation may be a function of experience with other providers, or the access and timeliness expectation set by the provider. If the customer experiences a wait that they judge as excessive (for example, on the phone or online), the wait itself becomes a kind of access denial. It doesn't matter if, after the excessive wait, access is provided and even easy, the wait becomes conflated with access.

Access by Service Providers to Customer Information

The information and ideas in this chapter have a singular focus on customers accessing their provider. However, it works in the other direction as well. Especially over the past two decades, access to customer information (e.g., demographics, purchase history, internet usage) has become highly desirable. Individual providers who are aware of the specifics of customer preferences and internet behavior can target specific customers with, for example, advertising that resonates with their past preferences and behavior. At a marketplace level, customer data has become a hot commodity. Some providers sell their customer information to other providers or data aggregators. The receivers of the data can process it and resell it, as well as conduct in-depth analysis to spot emerging trends in customer preference, purchase patterns, and internet behavior. For the individual customer interested in remaining anonymous, they must read the disclosure statements and, rather than clicking on "agree" without thinking, make an informed decision. There are also a variety of privacy tools in the marketplace. However, somewhat ironically, even some of these tools can be used to gather and then sell customer data.

Access and Usefulness

If the customer accesses service the way they want, using the means they want, but the service is not *useful in the way the customer wants*, the customer is likely to be dissatisfied. For example, the bank customer requests transaction history for a specific date range. The customer wants to use the transaction history for a specific period (e.g., mid-month to mid-month) to forecast their liquidity needs for the same period in the upcoming year. The bank can provide transaction history, but not for the specific range requested by the customer (the bank can only generate full month to full month history). The transaction history provided is accurate, available in a timely manner, and can be accessed via the customer's preferred channel (e.g., the bank's website) but, without considerable effort on the customer's part, the data can't be immediately used the way the customer wanted to use it.

Access and Responsiveness

Customers may view access as a fundamental feature of responsiveness. Not being able to access service when and how they want may be experienced by the customer as unresponsive. For example, the customer calls to service provider's contact center and gets the dreaded message, *"We are experiencing higher than expected call volumes. Your call will be answered in the order it was received."* The message might also include an estimated wait time, *"Your call will be answered within 5 minutes."* And, 5 minutes later, the customer is dumped into a set of menu prompts preceded by the message, *"Please listen to the entire message as our menu has changed."* Some customers will experience the situation above as both a denial of access and unresponsiveness.

Access and Problem Recovery

As stated a few times earlier, during problem recovery some customers may want access to a qualified human being. The operative word here is "qualified." Access to a person who is clearly unable to help during problem recovery compounds the initial problem. Likewise, if access during problem recovery is difficult, excessively complex, or overly time-consuming (e.g., repeatedly being put on hold), customers already dissatisfied with the problem are likely to become very dissatisfied. While some individual customers may want access to a person, *almost all* B2B customers want almost immediate access to a person when problems occur. Ideally, this means access to a CRM with the skills and authority to quickly solve the problem. It's worth repeating here and echoing it later, when problem recovery is examined in detail, service providers define their character and competence during problem recovery. Access is one of those defining elements. It must be acknowledged that the desire to reach a qualified human during problem recovery is not universal, and it may even be decreasing. Some customers want access to problem recovery via technology and will be dissatisfied if they are forced to deal with a person.

Some Examples of Access for Certain Types of Customers

The examples on the following page illustrate the diversity of customers and the types of access they might expect.

Customer Type	Provider Type	Access Type
Individual Customers (in general)	Service Providers	• Easy and fast access via the provider website and/or contact center • Access to a qualified person for problems (for some customers)
Financial Service End Customer	Financial Service Provider (e.g., Banks, Investment Firms)	• Easy and fast access via the provider website and/or contact center • Access to a qualified person for problems • For high net-worth customers, access to a CRM • Email access
Employee (all levels, all types)	Employee's Supervisor/ Manager	• Face-to-face access to supervisors/ managers • As more employees work at home, video (e.g., Zoom) access may replace or augment face-to-face access • Immediate access—face-to-face, phone, text, or email—to provide expert information or guidance (especially in contact centers where the customer may be on hold)
Employee (all levels, all types)	The Provider Company/ Corporation	Online (or on paper) access to policy, procedure, and FAQs (fast and easy to access and use)
Supervisor/ Manager	Employees	• Face-to-face, video, text, and email access • Employees make themselves accessible in exceptional circumstances (e.g., higher than expected work volume). Employee doesn't hide, resist, or complain
B2B Customer	B2B Provider	• Norm-referenced access (e.g., web, phone, email, video, face-to-face) • Access to a CRM during problem recovery

Continued →

Customer Type	Provider Type	Timeliness Type
Healthcare Patient	Healthcare Provider	• Face-to-face access to health professionals • Telemedicine access for routine or non-serious situations • Website access to test results, appointment scheduling, prescription refills
Healthcare Provider	Patient	Via face-to-face, paper form, web access; family history, prescriptions, habits (good/bad)
Employee's Colleagues	Employer	• General adherence to company rules/expectations about access expectations • Willingness and availability to help colleagues online or in person)
Community Member	Local Government	Norm referenced access regarding community services provided (typically via website, email broadcasts)
Local Government	Community Member	Community member conforms with access regulations/guidelines when using community services
Students	Teachers	• Face-to-face or computer mediated access to performance feedback (both scheduled and ad hoc) • Access to instruction via designated channels (e.g., face-to-face, internet synchronous/asynchronous)
Teacher	Students	Access to completed assignments in the required format (e.g., on paper, PDF, MS Word)

A Call to Action

Access as an integral ingredient of WACW can best be understood by applying it to a real customer and a real service provider. For example, if you are a senior manager of a large B2B service provider, the businesses you provide service to are clearly your customers; *they can feel satisfied or dissatisfied about what your organization does, and they can act based on that satisfaction or dissatisfaction.* However, the business-to-business relationship is different than that between an individual end-customer with their service provider. Individual customers can act quickly based on their satisfaction or dissatisfaction, while a business being serviced by a B2B provider will not be able to act as quickly. Business-to-business relationships tend to be quite complex to set up, implement, and may operate under restrictive contractual terms and obligations. Contractual relationships often limit the speed with which the relationship can be severed or expanded. On the positive side, a satisfied or very satisfied business customer may become a potent resource, or even a partner/advocate (e.g., helping to attract new business, publicly acknowledging their satisfaction).

If you are a business-to-business service provider, ask yourself, what does your B2B customer want relative to access? An example follows, but doing your own work will be much more meaningful and useful. (If you aren't a business provider, develop your individual customer's needs and wants relative to access.)

Your Business customers want...	Specific Example(s)
Periodic face-to-face access	Face-to-face customer meetings, often hosted by the provider, to participate in presentations and discussion about (for example): • Service performance relative to contractual standards • General and specific service problems • Service process continuous improvement efforts • Strategic planning
Telephone access	• Immediate or near immediate phone access to individuals or the service team • Callbacks within preset timeliness standards • 24/7 voicemail access • 24/7 emergency phone access

[89]

Your Business customers want...	Specific Example(s)
Access to a CRM	Immediate or near immediate access *to and from* a CRM • To report a problem • To remain current on problem recovery efforts • Project reporting • Performance discussion and reporting
Access via the internet	Internet access to include: • Dedicated website (perhaps even B2B customer specific) offering both informational and transactional service features • Email—group and individual • Texting • Live chat • Video access for group and individual, planned, and ad hoc meetings
Access problem prevention and resilience	Norm/marketplace referenced problem prevention in systems design, implementation, and ongoing operation, to prevent problems that include: • Viruses • Malicious software • Unauthorized access to proprietary information • Unauthorized access to personally identifying information • Ransomware Norm/marketplace referenced systems resilience—to "bounce back" from problems that include all the above plus systems/power outages
Access surveys	Surveys of both the B2B customer and their customers to assess emerging needs and satisfaction with access to the service provider

The preceding example of some of what B2B customers want from their B2B service provider in relation to access is only an example, and a generic one at that. Doing this for yourself in relation to one or more of your internal or external customers is an effort that will solidify your understanding of access as part of WACW. While access has always been important in the customer/provider relationship, because of increased access via technology, access is more critical than ever and will continue to evolve and rise in importance.

This discussion will now move on to the next element of What All Customers Want—Usefulness.

The usefulness of the cup is its emptiness.

—Bruce Lee

Information is only useful when it can be understood.

—Muriel Cooper

Information wants to be useful.

—Larry Walls

Chapter 5
Usefulness

A customer is anyone in a position to feel satisfied or
*dissatisfied about **usefulness** and can act based on*
their satisfaction or dissatisfaction.

Usefulness in relation to WACW is defined as the *customer's ability to use what the service provider delivers the way the customer wants to use it.* As with all the elements of WACW, usefulness looks easy to define and understand. And it is. But when examined in detail, it also has an underlying complexity that is not immediately apparent.

It may be tempting and even understandable to view usefulness as hierarchically less important than, for example, accuracy, timeliness, or access. Usefulness may seem too subjective or simply less foundational than the other elements of WACW. However, if the service provided was accurate, timely, and accessible, but not useful in the way the customer wanted, the service delivery is flawed and will likely lead to a dissatisfied customer. It should also be understood that, like all the elements of WACW, usefulness overlaps with the other elements. For example, inaccurate information is also useless (even dangerous). Late or out of date information is also useless. And useability, or ease of use, is a fundamental aspect of effective access. While these overlaps are present, service usefulness also has some features that can be unique.

In the preceding chapters about accuracy, timeliness, and access, the case was made that they are typically expected service outcomes or features and shortly after being made available, they are no longer a catalyst for increased customer satisfaction (with some exceptions, as noted in the preceding chapters). Usefulness also becomes expected, especially if it is part of a routine service delivery. However, if it is delivered on an *ad hoc*, situational basis, it may be more likely to engender longer term satisfaction—if it is judged useful by the customer. To fully understand this, it must first be understood that for the purposes of WACW, there are two types of usefulness.

1. The first type is ongoing, repetitive usefulness. The individual or B2B customers receives useful service (e.g., information, data, guidance) and the service is repeated at some fixed interval or if

the same service is requested by the customer periodically, but not necessarily according to a fixed schedule. For example, an institutional customer receives a monthly report used for understanding provider performance and for customer decision making. While there is an initial period in which the report is being designed, when it is finalized by both the customer and provider, it is deemed useful by the customer. At that point and moving forward in time until the report is revised, *its usefulness is expected and the report itself will not drive satisfaction up*, even though the content of the report may be satisfying or dissatisfying to the customer (e.g., reported provider performance rises or falls).

2. The second kind of usefulness is situational and for the customer, may be a single and unique service event (a "one-off"), or a service event that happens on an *ad hoc* and unpredictable basis. For example, the customer calls their service provider's contact center to acquire a pre-paid return label for a piece of unwanted merchandise. The customer will judge the call to the contact center and judge the usefulness of the requested label when it is received (telephone responsiveness will be discussed in detail in the next chapter). If the label is useful the way the customer wanted to use it, customer satisfaction may rise. If it isn't useful, dissatisfaction will likely be the result and even extreme dissatisfaction, if the process to acquire the label was onerous or time consuming. For some customers, a useful label was expected (e.g., because the customer had been through the process before) and no rise in satisfaction is likely. In contrast to this example, if customers call for information, data or guidance on a random basis, each service interaction will tend to be judged separately.

An additional note about repetitive and situational usefulness: While usefulness tends to be expected and therefore not a catalyst for increasing customer satisfaction, innovative or additive usefulness can produce increased customer satisfaction and even delight. For example, the bank offers its customers an easy to use fully customizable dashboard, thus allowing the customer to use the bank's website exactly the way they want to and to quickly revise the dashboard as the customer's interests or situation changes. Long-term, this feature may become expected, but especially if this capability is not offered by the customer's other service providers, this feature may result in sustained customer satisfaction.

Within the context of both repetitive and situational usefulness, there are several ways to define it further:

- Perfectly useful
- Useful enough
- Ease of use
- Useful as understandable
- Usefulness and utility

Perfectly Useful

Like precision accuracy and timeliness, a service delivery that is perfectly useful is one that matches *exactly* with what the customer wanted and their expectation for how they will use the delivered service. For example, there are several income tax preparation tools in the marketplace. The best of these offer input screens (often presented as simple questions) that align with, for example, 1099 forms. The tool asks for the figures contained in specific numbered items on the 1099. The customer simply finds the item number and types in the amount shown. One of the ways this tax preparation tool is perfectly useful is by using numbers in addition to language, so that customers don't need to do any analysis or interpretation.

Another example of a "perfectly useful" service delivery using the tax preparation tool from above is the ability to upload actual tax forms into the tool. For example, a customer can scan their W2 form and then upload it to the tax preparation tool. The tool then populates the customer's income tax form directly from the uploaded W2. The obvious and possible contradiction to this example of perfect usefulness occurs when the customer doesn't have access to a scanner. However, if the form can't be uploaded, as described above, the tax preparation tool uses the Q&A format linked to the tax form item number.

A third example will be used to illustrate both perfectly useful and less than perfectly useful. In this example, the institutional customer asks their institutional service provider to provide a report that can, upon receipt, immediately be inserted in a larger customer presentation to their (customer's) board of directors. The customer specifies both content and formatting requirements to their provider. One of the formatting requirements is that the report be provided in landscape versus portrait mode. The report is delivered. It's accurate, timely, and easily accessed, but it's provided in portrait mode, making it less than perfectly useful. By contrast, if all the other elements of WACW are addressed *and* the report is delivered in landscape mode, it can be judged as perfectly useful.

Useful Enough

Useful enough echoes earlier discussions of "Accurate Enough" and "Timely Enough." For some individual customers and B2B customers, service delivery doesn't need to be perfect to be useful. For example, the customer is planning their day and is expecting a package delivery, or a call-back from their service provider. Like the examples provided in the discussions of accuracy and timeliness, an approximation of the delivery or call-back time is useful enough for at least some customers (e.g., the call-back or package delivery is scheduled to occur between 4:00 p.m. EST and 5:00 p.m. EST). It must be acknowledged here that other customers may want greater precision to define the service delivery as useful. This may mean narrowing the service delivery time window (e.g., 15 minutes versus 1 hour), or it may mean the customer wants a Perfectly Useful service delivery (e.g., call-back or delivery at precisely 4:15 p.m. EST).

A second example helps illustrate the concept of useful enough. Even though a cooking recipe may be found in a book or online, it can be charactered as a service delivery (more accurately, self-service). Many recipes provide a mix of exact and approximate information. For example, the recipe calls for one tablespoon of salt and 1 of garlic, and a *pinch* of ginger and then goes on to say that the meat being cooked might range from 1.5 to 2.5 pounds. Even though there is a mix of exact and approximate measures, the recipe can be judged as useful enough.

A classic bell curve was used to illustrate Accurate Enough and Timely Enough. It can be used here to illustrate Useful Enough. The peak of the bell curve representing perfect usefulness but moving a few degrees off peak can be useful enough (i.e., sufficient usefulness to meet the customer's needs and not drive dissatisfaction). However, moving too far off the peak risks being defined by the customer as less than useful, or even useless (e.g., service delivery later than the window set as an expectation).

Ease of Use

Institutional and individual service providers that make their service easy to use will have a distinct advange in the marketplace over providers who's service is not easy to use or less easy to use. For example, a provider offereing web access to service that requires two to three "clicks" or screens to navigate to what customers want will do better than providers offering the same service, but require more than three clicks/screens.

> Unfortunately for some service providers offering website access, the customer will be comparing their experience of usefulness on the provider's site with other providers that may be much larger, having far greater technological resources, and experience. The small, niche service provider may be competing with Google or Amazon in terms of usefulness. At the same time, the small provider may, by virtue of being small, be nimbler. In any case, the small provider should seek expert assistance in the creation, maintenance, and ongoing development of their website. The small provider may have a niche product or service, but the tools and expertise presently available can make them competitive with much larger providers with much deeper pockets.

Ease of use is clearly and closely connected to access, as discussed in the previous chapter. Being accessible is part of a service being easy to use. However, there are clearly instances in which overall access is easy and fast, but the service itself is hard to use. For example, it's easy to access various government websites (e.g., Social Security, the IRS), but using the sites to achieve a goal is often anything but easy.

Ease of use is one of the hallmarks of effective customer service technology for both individual and B2B service providers. The design of both contact centers and provider websites, along with all other points of customer access, include ease of use as part of the developmental process. And it's not just a one-time goal, it's continuous and ongoing. In fact, as stated in the chapter on access, if provider systems were easy to use a few years ago, they are probably well behind the times in comparison to other providers who are constantly improving.

The preceding chapter concerning Access provides information about best practices for buiding and maintaining service provider websites, contact center technology, and individual provider phone service (e.g., the doctors office). The best practices for access also address ease of use and won't be repeated here. However, two best practices do bear repeating:

1. Providers developing, deploying, and maintaining web-based service delivery, customer contact centers, and provider phone service should use an expert. IT people are not necessarily experts, nor are graphic designers. Web design and call center technology have become their own disciplines, requiring highly specialized expertise and experience in designing ease of use into customer service technologies.

2. The second-best practice under access that applies to ease of use that bears repeating is enabling the customer experiencing a problem who wants to reach a live person to easily do so. Other customers will define *useful* in the context of a service problem as a well-designed and easy-to-use provider website or some other technology. It is important to remember that *providers define their true character and culture by how they handle problems. And customers decside what is easy and useful.*

> **A personal example.** During the peak years of my career, I traveled a lot. I was willing to pay extra for a credit card that offered me ease of use in terms of the ability to quickly speak with someone if I needed help or a problem occurred. Early on, I did have to say my account number to be connected, but after I did so, within a brief period I was speaking with a person. Not a front-line CSR. The many times I used this feature, I was always connected to a more senior person who made it easy for me to get what I called for (e.g., solved my problem). It's easy to imagine this technology improving to the point that the provider's response technology will recognize my number, my voice, and/or my face and that the person taking the call will have all my information before I say anything, perhaps even anticipating my reason for calling. This level of ease of use will give the service provider a competitive advantage, at least until all providers can deliver this level of customer satisfaction. However, it should be remembered that the last thing some customers want when making an inquiry or experiencing a problem is to speak to a person. Instead, they want easy-to-use technology (often via a handheld device).

Useful as Understandable

Information, data, or guidance/directions provided to the customer must be understandable to be useful. Further, different customers will have different—sometimes very different—capabilities about understanding.

There is a significant amount of research about the conveyance of information, specifically with regard to the written word. The Flesch—Kincaid Grade Level is one of the most widely used tools for assessing reading level. (Most reading level tests use a word total, sentence count, along with a syllable count among other factors to compute reading level). It's suggested that text aimed at the general public should aim for about an 8th grade reading level. Information aimed at specialized users (e.g., IT manuals, physicians) can be written at a higher level, reflecting the expertise of users (customers).

To be understandable and therefore useful, information, data, or guidance/directions provided to the customer via the internet (e.g., provider website), over the phone (e.g., via a provider contact center), a face-to-face meeting, or a video conference should all have certain attributes. The following is representational of those attributes:

- Easy Website Access—No more than three "clicks"/three screens to useful information on a website; no more than three rings to a pickup over the phone (even if the pickup is automated).

- Concise—Be brief. Brevity in the written word is achieved through successive editing, in the spoken word through practice.

- Clear—Simple words with no ambiguity. It's wise, when giving directions, to organize the content in chronological order.

- Complete—Leave nothing out. This can be a threat to concision, but again, especially when giving directions, the provider must be thorough.

- Correct—This may seem obvious, but editing for accuracy in the written word is especially important.

- In written material, it's okay to use sentence fragments for lists.

- Provide FAQs (Frequently Asked Questions) and a way to make contact to ask addtional questions.

Over the phone, manage verbal mannerisms (covered in more detail in Responsiveness, Chapter 6):

- Pace/speed
- Tone of voice
- Clarity of the spoken word
- Presence/absence of an accent (regional/global)
- Pauses
- Nonsense words/fillers (e.g., err, umm)

Face-to-Face (covered in more detail in Responsiveness, Chapter 6):

- Facial expression
- Gestures
- Eye contact
- Repetitive (distracting) movement

Video conference:

- Have a mututally understood agenda (even if it is just one item)
- Set time parameters ("this is planned as a 30-minute call")
- Mute (yourself) if you are not speaking
- Eliminate background distractions and distracting behavior
- Look at the camera, not your screen, when speaking

It's worth making a special note to assess customer understanding in real time on a phone call or during a face-to-face meeting. Even when the customer doesn't come out and say, "I don't understand," there are often clues to watch and listen for. Over the phone, if the customer asks the provider to repeat content, that may be a sign of misunderstanding. Also, over the phone, customer tone can communicate uncertainty or confusion. Face-to-face uncertainty may be communicated by a change in facial expression or the customer shaking their head. If the provider thinks the customer doesn't understand the information, data, or guidance being delivered, they must politely check in with the customer. It's easy for the provider to forget that they may be delivering the same service multiple times per day or even per hour, but for the customer, this may be the first time they are hearing the information, data, or guidance.

Usefulness and Utility

Interestingly, the two words usefulness and utility, while both are nouns and clearly reflective of one another, do have distinct attributes. Usefulness is, "the quality of being useful." Utility overlaps with that defining attribute and then has specialized meaning. For example, in economics, utility is "the ability of a commodity to satisfy needs and wants." Utility can also refer to the electric or water company. In computer technology, utility refers to software designed to perform a single or very limited number of tasks (e.g., antivirus software, compression tools).

For the purposes of WACW, using the word *useful* makes sense. It's the quality of being useful. However, it's worth knowing the economic definition of utility—satisfy needs and wants—since it overlaps so clearly with the usefulness definition (i.e., use the service the way the customer *wants* to use it). Using the electric or water companies as a simile also makes sense, since useful information from the service provider is most often expected, like power and water from the utilities. Also, like a power outage, providing non-useful service to the customer can be dissatisfying, even traumatic. Finally, using a computer utility as a metaphor also makes sense in relation to repetitive usefulness—its usefulness is automatic and predictable.

Usefulness in Relation to the Other Elements of What All Customers Want (WACW)

Usefulness and Accuracy

As stated as this chapter began, inaccurate information, data, or guidance is both incorrect and useless. It may even be dangerous since decisions or actions made based on an error will necessarily be wrong. For example, an airline pilot expecting perfectly accurate and useful information about weather conditions ahead or landing instructions, but receiving incorrect and therefore useless information, could lead to catastrophic results. Likewise, a doctor expecting perfectly accurate and useful test results, but receiving incorrect data instead, could make decisions dangerous to their patient.

Usefulness and Timeliness

Similar to accuracy, information, data, or guidance received later than expected or needed may also be useless. The word "may" is used intentionally here. Late information, data, or guidance may be timely enough and thus, useful enough. For example, the customer receiving information late by only a small margin may still find it useful (e.g., a customer receiving a provider report a few minutes to a few hours late may still be able to use the information, if the actual use of the report is targeted at the next day). In stark contrast, in some cases, even being a little late can be judged as completely useless (e.g., a commodities trader tracking commodity pricing may not be able to use data provided even a few seconds to a few minutes late).

Usefulness and Access

If the customer can't access the information, data, or guidance they want, they can't use it. Likewise, if the service sought can't easily be accessed, then ease of use is inherently reduced. If the information, data, or guidance can be easily accessed, it's still no guarantee that it will be useful. Like the example provided in the chapter on Access, the customer may be able to easily access their bank, but the bank may or may not be able to provide useful results to the customer— the way the customer wanted to use the results (e.g., the bank provides the customer with transaction data, but not in the format or order the customer wants to use it). It is fair to say that inaccessible service is useless and useless or hard-to-use service can be defined as inaccessible.

Usefulness and Responsiveness

The customer receiving useful information, data, or guidance is fundamental to defining responsiveness. Likewise, not receiving useful service, or less than fully useful service, can be experienced by the customer as unresponsive. And the customer may not know whether the service received was useful or not until after the service interaction. For example, the customer, in reviewing their credit card statement, finds a charge they don't recognize and calls the credit card contact center or uses the credit card company's website. In either case, the customer is given guidance about how to research the transaction and, if necessary, dispute the bill. The customer follows the instructions, but still can't identify the source of the charge and is left with the arbitrary (unsupported) decision about whether or not to dispute the bill. In this example, the customer could not use the information provided the way they wanted to and only found out after the interaction with the provider, making the service interaction both unresponsive and useless.

Usefulness and Problem Recovery

During problem recovery, the customer's sensitivity during the process rises in comparison to a typical service encounter. One way to define usefulness in the context of problem recovery is that the problem was fixed, the way the customer wanted. In addition, usefulness during problem recovery would include easy to use steps that the customer can take to solve or contribute to the solution of the problem. On the flip side, if the problem recovery process is complex and demanding, the customer may experience a compounding of the initial problem. Providers have come a long way in making problem recovery easy for the customer. Many have recognized what has repeatedly been said here; that *service providers define their character and culture by how they address problems*. To return to an example used earlier, the prepaid return labels (RMA labels) have made the problem recovery process easier and more useful. It should also be noted that the provider can also find the problem recovery process useful. At best, they learn from their mistakes, making the mistakes highly useful.

Some Examples of Usefulness for Certain Types of Customers

The table below provides examples that illustrate the diversity of customers and the types of usefulness they might expect.

Customer Type	Provider Type	Usefulness Type
Individual Customers (in general)	Service Providers	• Easy to use provider website and/or contact center (e.g., menu prompts sequencing reflects most frequent customer questions/actions) • Easy/understandable sequential steps for problem recovery (on the website or from the contact center)

Continued →

Customer Type	Provider Type	Usefulness Type
Financial Service End Customer	Financial Service Provider (e.g., Banks, Investment Firms)	• Perfectly useful and understandable financial/account reports • Easy to use access channel to ask a question (phone, chat, etc.) • Easy to use instructions for initiating the problem recovery process (e.g., with a service provider representative and/or via the provider website)
Employee (all levels, all types)	Employee's Supervisor/ Manager	• Easy to use feedback (e.g., clear, concise, examples provided; expectations understandable and, if appropriate, quantifiable) • Perfectly useful communication channels (e.g., technology) for reaching out to the supervisor during or directly after an interaction with an individual customer (e.g., to obtain authorization, direction, expert opinion)
Employee (all levels, all types)	The Provider Company/ Corporation	Online (or on paper) access to policy procedure and FAQs—fast and easy to access and either perfectly useful or useful enough
Supervisor/ Manager	Employees	• Employee work product or special tasks are easy to use and understandable • Employee-generated reports are perfectly useful in relation to quantified data and understandable in relation to narrative information
B2B Customer	B2B Provider	• Norm referenced ease of use (e.g., web, phone, email, video, face-to-face) • Easy access to a CRM during or web-based tools for problem identification and recovery

Continued →

Customer Type	Provider Type	Usefulness Type
Healthcare Patient	Healthcare Provider	• Perfectly useful diagnostic test results • Directions to patient are understandable and at least useful enough to enable patient compliance • Easy to use website access to test results, appointment scheduling, prescription refills
Healthcare Provider	Healthcare Patient	Understandable and useful enough patient self-reporting (perfectly useful and precisely accurate may not be a reasonable expectation for most patients)
Employee's Colleagues	Employee	• Employee provides useful support to colleagues • Employee written and verbal communication is understandable (e.g., clear, concise, complete)
Community Member	Local Government	Norm referenced ease of use regarding community services provided (typically via website, email broadcasts)
Local Government	Community Member	Community member input to local government is understandable—not entirely subjective, self-serving—and useful enough
Students	Teachers	• Useful enough access to performance feedback (both scheduled and ad hoc) • Perfectly useful access to instruction via designated channels (e.g., face-to-face, internet synchronous/asynchronous
Teachers	Students	Completed assignments in the format (e.g., on paper, PDF, MS Word) that can be easily used by the teacher

A Call to Action

Usefulness as an integral ingredient of WACW can best be understood by applying it to a real customer and a real service provider. For example, if you are running a small business out of your home and your contact with customers is primarily via the website you created and limited phone access, ask yourself, what does your customer want relative to usefulness?

Your customers want...	Specific Example(s)
Easy to Use Website	Website developed and maintained to conform with best practices (see "Access Via the Internet" in Chapter 4), for example: • Simple, consistent, and attractive • Designed for desktop/laptop computers as well as handheld devices • Intuitive navigation • Simple effective search functionality • Clear Call to Action (CTA)
Easy to Use Ordering, Payment, and Return Options	• Allow "Check out as visitor" (Forcing signing up as a user makes the entire process less easy. Encourage, but don't force.) • Offer an array of payment options (e.g., Quick Books online, PayPal, Ramp, Credit Card, Apple Pay, Google Pay) • Build RMA (Return Merchandize Authorization) label creation into your website.
Easy to Use and Understandable Phone Access (limited)	• Easy to use phone number (perhaps using a mnemonic device, e.g., 1-800-Call-Jane, but also give the number) • Recorded announcement begins with a statement that the website may be faster • Menu prompts given in order of most to least frequent customer need/want • Person answering speaks clearly, demonstrates understanding, etc. (see Chapter 6, Responsiveness)
Usefulness Surveys	Surveys of both customers to assess current and emerging needs and satisfaction with usefulness delivered by service provider website and other points of contact.

The example of what customers want from their small business service provider in relation to usefulness is generic. Doing this for yourself in relation to one or more of your internal or external customers is an effort that will solidify your understanding of usefulness as part of WACW. Usefulness has always been important in the customer/provider relationship, but because of the often-bewildering array of technology channels, usefulness is more critical than ever and will continue to rise in importance.

Now, the discussion will move on to the next element of What All Customers Want, Responsiveness.

> *Listening is not waiting to talk.*
>
> —Axiom

> **Customer:** *"I'm really getting frustrated."*
> **CSR:** *"I know how you feel."*
> **Customer:** (Getting angry) *"No you don't."*
>
> —On the Phone

Chapter 6
Responsiveness

*A customer is anyone in a position to feel satisfied or dissatisfied about **responsiveness** and can act based on their satisfaction or dissatisfaction.*

Responsiveness is first defined in relation to the other elements of WACW. Thus, responsiveness is accuracy, timeliness, access, usefulness, and when necessary, effective problem recovery. A failure to deliver one or more of the other elements of WACW will automatically make the service delivery unresponsive to the customer. But responsiveness is also more than the effective delivery of the other elements of WACW. It's much more. It is actively demonstrating an understanding of the customer's perspective. *It's the demonstration of empathy.* In the case of face-to-face, telephone, video, and even email, responsiveness is also, among other behaviors, the provider's tone of voice, their ability to communicate clearly, their ability to respond effectively to emotions expressed by the customer, and many other behaviors. This chapter will describe and provide examples of responsive behavior, as well as placing these behaviors in the context of face-to-face, telephone, video, email, and other computer mediated interactions.

What about responsiveness of technology? The preceding chapters on WACW speak to this question. Specifically, the chapters on *access* and *usefulness* describe best practices (e.g., for Website design) that are also the attributes of responsive technology. Moving forward in time, the continued pursuit of artificial intelligence may produce technology that behaves in a way indistinguishable from a human being, and thus, responsiveness of technology may have a natural behavioral aspect. But we're not there yet. Thus, this chapter will focus on human providers serving their human customers.

Behavioral responsiveness can be a long-term satisfier:
While the other elements of WACW tended, over the long-term, to be expected and thus, even when delivered successfully, not be a source rising satisfaction. (But when not delivered effectively, they are a potent source of dissatisfaction and possibly extreme dissatisfaction.) Responsiveness is different. Certainly, unresponsive behavior can

drive dissatisfaction. Impolite, rude behavior, speaking too quickly to be understood, not listening, cutting the customer off, are just a few of the behaviors that can drive dissatisfaction, even when the other elements of WACW are delivered. By contrast, polite, professional, friendly behavior, clear speaking voice, the demonstration of empathy and patience with the customer, when combined with the effective delivery of the other WACW elements, will likely produce satisfaction and even extreme satisfaction. The fundamental difference between exhibiting effective responsiveness and the other elements of WACW is that highly responsive behavior is *always* valued by many customers and may be a source of continuing satisfaction. Stated another way, *customers don't take a truly responsive service provider for granted.* Every time they interact with a provider demonstrating responsive behaviors, especially the demonstration of empathy, their satisfaction is maintained or grows. Talking with a pleasant, competent person who listens and helps is always a pleasure.

> **The Turing Test:** Named after Alan Turing, the test is a procedure to determine whether a computer is capable of thinking like a human being and responding to certain stimuli in a manner equivalent to or indistinguishable from a human. As of this writing, no computer has ever passed the Turing Test.

Before defining responsiveness, non-responsiveness will be described. Doing so will bring responsive behavior into sharp focus.

What *Isn't* Responsive?

1. In a face-to-face, phone conversation, or video meeting, the following phrases, which are in common and frequent use, are upon examination, unresponsive:
   - *"I understand."*
   - *"I hear what you are saying."*
   - *"I know exactly what you're saying."*
   - *"I know what you mean."*
   - *"I know how you feel."*

2. Even more unresponsive:
   - *"Welcome to my world."*
   - *"Been there, done that."*

3. It gets worse. The phrases that follow are not only unresponsive, but they are also likely to irritate the customer more than they already are. Not necessarily with external customers, but more often with internal customers (e.g., a supervisor speaking with a front-line employee) the following phrases might be heard:

- *"Just relax."*
- *"You have to calm down."*
- *"Don't feel that way."*
- *"You shouldn't feel that way."*
- *"Don't take it personally."*

> With literally thousands of students over the years, I've tried to illustrate the ineffectiveness of phrases like "I understand," by asking a question. "How many people in your life understand you?" The answer is seldom zero, but it is most often only a few people. I then ask my students to contrast the frequency of hearing or saying "I understand" with the experience of being understood. The answer is obvious. ***Understanding is claimed far more often than it is true.***

Care needs to be taken here not to condemn the users of some of the first list of phrases above. For example, the CSR saying, *"I hear what you're saying"* to a customer may have the best of intentions. Ironically, some of the phrases in the first list that are labeled as unresponsive are encouraged and even taught to customer facing personnel (e.g., CSRs are encouraged to say, *"I understand"*). Again, the people encouraging the use of such phrases are not doing so with ill intentions. They recognize that being listened to and being understood are important to customers. *But making the claim of understanding should not be confused with demonstrating understanding.* And that's the problem with the unresponsive phrases; they claim understanding without offering proof. There should be little disagreement that the phrases from list number two above are simply dismissive and rude. List number three provides phrases telling the customer (e.g., front line employee), how they should feel rather than reflecting on the feeling they've expressed. Not only might these phrases be experienced as patronizing or rude, but they are also ineffective and even counterproductive (e.g., telling someone to calm down will often have the opposite of the intended effect.)

Responsiveness Channels

In the previous chapters, each element of WACW was defined and then illustrated by describing the different forms or types of the element. For example, the various types of accuracy included precision accuracy, accurate enough, accuracy as the truth, and so on. In this chapter, responsiveness will be further defined and described in relation to the setting or channel in which responsive or unresponsive behavior is demonstrated. The settings are:

- Face-to-face
- Over the phone
- Conference calls and video conferencing
- Email, text, chat, etc.

Face-to-Face Responsiveness[*]

Examples of face-to-face encounters between a customer and service provider are seemingly endless. The customer goes into the provider's "store" (whatever and wherever the store is). The patient goes to the doctor's office or the dentist. The B2B customer visits the B2B provider's office for a one-on-one or group meeting. The B2B provider visits the B2B customer's office. The bank customer goes into the bank's lobby to see a bank officer. The list goes on, the grocery store, the pharmacy, the restaurant, the classroom, the internal customer's work setting.

What all these encounters have in common is face-to-face, close physical proximity between the customer and the provider. Further, what all these encounters also have in common are the behaviors of both the provider and the customer. These behaviors include verbal mannerisms (e.g., tone, pace, sounds like er, uhm), visual signals/cues (e.g., eye contact, nodding, distance), and verbal content (e.g., word usage, question asking, responding with or without listening/ empathy).

---

[*] Most of the behavioral skills described as responsive in face-to-face communication with customers readily apply to providing customer service over the phone, during conference calls, and video conferencing.

What follows are *some* of the best practices for face-to-face responsiveness demonstrated by the service provider and experienced by the customer.[*]

> At this writing, the pandemic has been with us for a number of years. There is some hope that the pandemic will become endemic (like seasonal flu), returning us to a somewhat normal state. But certainly, work at home, lockdowns, quarantine, and business closures have profoundly changed the frequency and the quality of face-to-face communication between customers and providers. It's safe to say that, during the pandemic, the frequency of face-to-face communication has decreased dramatically. And as customers do venture out, the prudent customer and provider may be wearing masks and maintaining social distancing, thus taking away many visual signals/cues. Some theorists think that after the pandemic becomes endemic, communication will return to pre-pandemic practices. Others think that some things have changed forever (e.g., the acceptance of work at home). Whatever happens, there will still be some level of face-to-face communication between providers and their customers.

What to Listen For

To be predictably judged as responsive or highly responsive, the service provider in face-to-face communication with their customers should *listen* to the customer, listening for:

- **Words used by the customer.** The customer's vocabulary can give the service provider clues to the customer's level of knowledge or lack of knowledge about what is being discussed, thus enabling the service provider to present information in a way the customer will understand.

- **Words or phrases used repetitively by the customer.** Repetition or themes from the customer may tell the service provider what is important to the customer. For example, if the customer repeatedly talks about frustration or satisfaction with the provider's website, this may mean that web access is

---

[*] What follows in this section and chapter is derived from the author's experience and the work of several interpersonal communication skills researchers, theorists, and practitioners. Among them are Carl Rogers, Robert R. Carkhuff, and Albert Mahrabian.

[113]

hierarchically more important to the customer than other elements of WACW (this may be situational or constant over time).

- **Feelings expressed by the customer.** For example, a customer who says they are "a little concerned" about something, may be very different than the customer who says they are "very concerned." The service provider should also be aware that some customers may be hyperbolic (exaggerating their expression of feeling), while others may understate their emotions. Service providers who have a long-term relationship with their customers (e.g., doctors, supervisors, teachers) will become increasingly astute in judging the emotional state of their customers.

- **Beliefs or convictions.** The customer comes to the service interaction with their own point of view. They may believe certain things (e.g., the provider puts service above profit or vice versa). They may have certain convictions (e.g., the service provider is truthful or never truthful). Customer convictions and beliefs don't have to be true to exert a powerful influence. Service providers should be listening for customer beliefs and convictions.

> It is an anecdotal observation, but more than a few medical doctors I've worked with have remarked that it is often the patient with the most severe problem who makes the fewest demands and expresses only modest emotional concern. In stark contrast, the patient with the fairly trivial health problem may make the most demands and express strong emotions. The smart, experienced physician considers this phenomenon when making their inferences, although in no case would an effective physician act *only* on generalities or anecdotal evidence.

- **The customer's tone of voice and other verbal mannerisms.** Emphasizing certain words or phrases may tell the service provider about the customer's perception about what is important, and the underlying feeling associated with the customer's expression. (More on this topic follows in this section.)

- **The customer's frame of reference.** Reflected by some or all of the customer behaviors listed above, the customer's frame of reference are the values and assumptions the customer brings to the interaction. For example, some customers want all the details, while others want the "big picture." Some customers don't express a lot of feelings, others "wear their feelings on their sleeve." Listening for the customer's frame of reference gives the service provider a broad and general understanding of the customer which, in turn, allows the provider to demonstrate their understanding—*all too rare and very powerful.*

Body Language

To be predictably judged as responsive or highly responsive, the service provider in face-to-face communication with their customers should demonstrate the following *physical* behaviors (AKA body language):

- **Make eye contact**—Consistent, but not staring. If the customer is clearly uncomfortable with eye contact (e.g., can't return eye contact), decrease the frequency.

- **Manage your facial expression**—An open and generally positive expression. Echoing the expression of the customer can be effective and a kind of visual empathy. Be careful not to express extreme emotion (e.g., surprise, frustration, anger) via facial expression.

- **Incline toward the customer**—a *slight* incline toward the customer while seated or standing shows interest and attention.

- **Supportive gestures**—Nodding to show nonverbal agreement, hands open, relaxed posture (not too stiff/rigid), etc.

- **Find the right distance**—Neither too close, nor too far away. An extended arm's length at least. (During the pandemic, the phrase "social distancing" came into wide use and meant maintaining a 6-foot distance from others.)

- **Eliminate distracting behavior**—Fiddling with pen or paper, drumming fingers, constant movement of any kind (e.g., foot tapping).

- **Over a desk/conference table**—All of the behaviors above, moving, eye contact, and slight incline to the person speaking.

- **Observe others**—Look for the presence or absence of all the physical behaviors above being demonstrated by the customer, allowing the observer to make inferences about the customer's level of agreement, understanding, resistance, etc.

Important Note: Any one or all the physical behaviors listed above will, if taken to the extreme, produce the opposite of the desired result and become unresponsive, even irritating to the customer (e.g., staring, too much incline, nodding too much, too quickly).

Verbal Mannerisms

To be predictably judged as responsive or highly responsive, the service provider in face-to-face communication with their customers should demonstrate or minimize the following *verbal mannerisms*:

- **Manage Pace/Speed**—The average person speaks at a rate of 100 to 130 words per minute. By contrast, professional speakers and advertisers may speed up to 150 to 160 words per minute. Providers in face-to-face communication should adjust their pace depending on the customer's reaction:

  — Slowing down, if the customer asks the provider to do so, asks a question that has already been answered, asks the provider to repeat, or customer tone indicates uncertainty or confusion, etc.

  — Speeding up slightly, if the customer indicates impatience (e.g., *"I know, get on with it."*), asks the provider to speed up, asks the provider to *"just hit the highlights,"* etc.

- **Tone of Voice**—While inherently difficult to describe, it is a reasonable axiom to say that if tone contradicts content, tone will carry the message to the customer.[*] For example, an impatient or even unfriendly tone will overwhelm the provider's verbal content. Two ways to get input to develop effective tone are: 1) The provider gets input from colleagues about their tone, and 2) The

---

[*] Albert Mahrabian authored several worthwhile books on nonverbal communication. While his books originally came out a few decades ago, they remain a reliable and useful resource. One example: Mehrabian, Albert, "Nonverbal Communication," Published in 2017 by Transaction Publishers.

provider records their voice in various conversations (e.g., stressful, easy, informational).

- **Manage Volume (loudness)**—Being easy to hear is an advantage to both provider and customer. Speaking too softly will often mean that the customer must ask the provider to repeat themselves, or even more directly, the customer has to ask the provider to "speak up." It's both a stereotype and a truth that older people are more likely to have hearing loss. Speaking up, especially with customers over 50, makes sense. In contrast, speaking too loudly can be quite irritating. Look and listen for signals from the customer (e.g., leaning in, leaning back, asking for repetition) to find the right volume for the customer.

- **Manage Regional Accents**—An extreme accent can pose a barrier to responsiveness if the accent becomes the focus of the customer's attention. Extreme accents can also be a barrier to customer understanding and the customer may or may not acknowledge the problem. Voice training can provide an offset, as can recording the provider's voice. (A case can be made that an accent can be an asset to responsiveness. However, this is less likely than an extreme accent posing a liability.)

- **Manage Verbal Utterances**—Utterances can be effective. Like periodically nodding one's head to acknowledge listening can be useful. However, frequent use of "err," "uhm," and the like can be distracting. Injecting certain repetitive words can also be distracting. Frequently saying, "you know (*ya know*)," "just," and "like" can have the same distracting quality as repetitive utterances as well as being bereft of intrinsic meaning.

- **Use Silence**—Waiting, giving the customer time to collect their thoughts to present their perspective can be very effective. All too often, silence is experienced as uncomfortable and, as a result, customers and providers keep talking, when taking time to think is exactly the right thing to do. Waiting, practicing being silent, will make it less uncomfortable and more productive.

Verbal Behavior

To be predictably judged as responsive or highly responsive, the service provider in face-to-face communication with their customers should demonstrate the following *verbal behavior*:

[117]

- **Effective Questions**—Asking the right question for the customer and the customer's situation is part of being responsive. The provider often needs information from the customer to provide service. An effective, responsive provider develops an understanding of various types of questions for different customer situations, including:

  — *Direct Questions*—They tend to yield a very focused answer from the customer, often a single word or piece of data (e.g., *"What was the date of the transaction you want me to research?", "What time did you arrive at your desk?", "Do you want me to explain the details about X?"* Direct questions help the provider obtain the essential facts to begin delivering service. Also, using direct and easy-to-answer questions can be a good way to get a conversation going.

  NOTE: In telephone service, technology is reducing the need for asking the customer verification questions. It is prepopulating the provider's screen based on the customer's call-in number or other information gathered before the call begins. At the same time, the CSR may need to ask one or more "qualifying" questions for security purposes and this can irritate some customers. Reminding these customers that questions are asked "to protect their account" may help.

  — *Forced Choice Direct Questions*—Offers the customer a limited array of options, all of which can be addressed by the provider. *"Do you want me to send the material to you via Next Day FedEx, UPS, or USPS Priority Mail?"* Use the foregoing instead of, *"How do you want me to send the material to you?"* The answer to the latter question may not be possible for the provider (e.g., hand-delivered by courier).

  — *Open-Ended Questions*—*" What can I do for you?" "How can I help you?"* Both of these questions are open-ended and in widespread use. *"What do you want to happen?" "What's your goal?"* These are also open-ended questions, allowing the customer to express their point of view or their goal.

  NOTE: It must be acknowledged that open-ended questions can be risky in both face-to-face and telephone communication. The primary risk is lengthening the service interaction. A second risk is that the customer will take the interaction in a direction the service provider can't address (e.g., customer asks for qualitative advice the provider can't give). Often, at the end of the service interaction, the provider will ask, *"Is there anything else I can help you with?"* Instead of this open-ended question, the provider might instead say, *"Have I answered all of your questions about X?"* which is a direct question and may then allow the provider to wind down the service interaction.

— *Reflective Questions*—This type of question shows that the provider is listening and solicits additional information. For example, *"You said you're not happy with when you receive our report, since it's too close to your deadline. What would be the ideal time to get the report, or a time range that would work for you?"* (There will be more on *reflecting* in the next segment.)

— *Leading Questions*—As the term implies, the leading question pushes the customer toward the answer the provider wants, thus, it is not really a question since it doesn't yield any new information. A leading question can also be destructive. If the customer feels that the provider is being manipulative, the customer may become quite irritated, even if they don't express it. For example, a supervisor (provider) giving feedback to an employee (an internal customer) says, *"You know it's important to be at your desk and ready to take calls at 9:00 a.m., don't you?"* This question is at once patronizing and ineffective in getting information from the customer (in this case, the employee).

Listening and Reflecting

- **Demonstrating listening skills and understanding by using a reflection.** Instead of claiming to understand (e.g., *"I understand,"* *"I hear what you're saying"*), reflecting what the customer has said provides proof that the provider has listened. As asserted earlier, being with someone who really listens is regrettably rare. If the provider develops the skills for listening and reflecting, the probability of the customer judging the provider as responsive increases significantly. There are various forms of Reflecting:

  - *Verbatim Reflection*—This is repeating back what the customer has said. While verbatim reflecting has a limited application, it is still a critical skill in some circumstances. For example, a pilot or naval officer receiving specific instructions regarding course and speed will repeat back what they've heard to eliminate any chance of misunderstanding (achieving perfect mutual understanding). When Precision accuracy is required, as described in Chapter 2, this may also be a situation in which the verbatim reflection is useful. For example, when the customer provides their address, phone number, or other short numeric or demographic information, a verbatim reflection by the provider may be called for. However, verbatim reflections can be inappropriate when the customer expresses longer, more narratively oriented verbal content.

— *Interchangeable Reflection*—This kind of reflection captures everything the customer has said but changes the order and words used. This kind of reflection is useful when the customer has provided narrative information (e.g., a "story" with a number of elements—a goal, a problem, a belief or value, general or specific request for help).

— *Summary Reflection*—This kind of reflection captures the essence (e.g., main points, goal) of what the customer has said, but may leave out some of the narrative content.

— *Reflection of Feeling*—This reflection can be combined with a summary reflection or stand on its own. The word(s) used to reflect feeling can come from the customer or from the provider's understanding of what the customer has said.

In the table provided on page 122, alternative feeling words are given. The provider listens to understand what word seems to fit for the customer—often based on tone of voice. For example, just from the written example, it would be wrong for the provider to say, *"You're terrified..."* or, on the opposite side of the scale, *"You're just a little concerned..."*.

— *Self-Disclosure*—This kind of reflection involves the service provider *briefly* describing an experience they've had that compares favorably to the customer's situation. While useful, this kind of reflection runs the risk of moving the focus to the provider versus the customer, but it does show a level of empathy (more on empathy later).

— *Interpretative/Additive Reflection*—This goes beyond what the customer has said into what is meaningful for the customer, the customer's goal(s), or an additive insight based on the provider's understanding of what the customer said and, in a face-to-face interaction, based on the customer's verbal manner (e.g., tone) and physical behaviors (e.g., facial expression).

The table on the following page provides examples of types of possible reflections.

Reflecting Examples

Customer says: *I'm in the middle of moving to a new house and, as you're aware, it's also tax season. I want to make sure that you have my new address and the timing of the move so that I get my statements as fast as possible. I know I can get most of it from your website, but I need to have physical copies mailed to me.*

Types of Possible Reflections

Interchangeable Reflection	Summary Reflection	Reflection of Feeling	Self-Disclosure	Additive Reflection
You want us to mail physical copies of your statements that you need for tax purposes, and you want your statements as soon as possible. You're also in the middle of moving, so you want to make sure we have your new address and the point at which you'll be receiving mail at that address.	*You want to make sure that your statements are sent to the right address at the right time.*	*You're [worried, concerned, afraid] that if we don't get your address and the timing of your move right, you won't get your statements as soon as possible.*	*You're moving and worried about getting your mail. I moved recently and it took a while for my mail to catch up with me because I didn't get ahead of it, which is what you're doing now in terms of your statements.*	*You've got a lot going on and you do not want the added worry of not getting your statements. You want to be 100% confident about getting your statements ASAP to the right address.*

Additional Notes about the Reflecting Skill

(Worth the additional focus since reflecting is at the heart of being Responsive.)

1. If the Interchangeable Reflection in the example above seems too long and unnecessary, that may be true for some customers. But for others, an interchangeable reflection provides the proof that the provider has listened and understood and thus, makes the customer more confident than if the provider simply asked, *"What's your new address"?*

2. The interpretative or additive reflection can be dangerous. It can be wrong, or sound wrong to the customer. It can also sound like a leading question. At the same time, this kind of reflection can be very powerful because, if effective, it taps into and articulates the meaning or goal behind the content expressed by the customer. The ability to craft an effective interpretive/additive reflection is a function of the skills and experience of the individual service provider and their willingness to focus fully on the customer—not always easy in a chaotic work environment.

3. Notice that all the examples of reflections begin with the word "You" (or "You're", "You've"). While reflecting must be genuine and immediate and there are no "tricks," beginning a reflection with "You..." is a way to help anchor what comes next to what the other person said, the other person's perspective. That said, a reflection does not have to always begin with "You." For example, still reflecting the same customer used in the previous examples, *"Moving is complicated—lots of moving parts. Especially when you're expecting important mail, you want to make sure everything is set up just right."* The "you're" is still there, but later on in the reflection.

4. Should the provider always reflect? *Absolutely not.* Arbitrarily inserting a reflection each time the customer says something wouldn't just be unresponsive, it would likely become very irritating to the customer. (**Remember:** Repeating what someone has just said is a kid's game, intended as an irritant.) At the same time, an effective service provider should be able to reflect at will and then choose when to verbalize it (e.g., when it would be useful to move the conversation forward, when the customer has presented facts/numbers, when the customer has expressed a goal or a strong emotion).

[123]

5. It is important to understand that a reflection may be entirely correct but may also be denied by the customer. For example, the customer expresses anger, the provider reflects that feeling, and the customer denies being angry. While this can be a challenge to the individual provider, at least with external customers, the provider must stay with the customer. This may mean asking more questions and reflecting content through multiple iterations. However, with some internal customers (e.g., a supervisor interacting with an employee), the provider (supervisor) may simply present their perspective and work with the employee toward mutual understanding—even if mutual agreement is not achieved.

6. Other than the verbatim reflection of numbers, specific names, or facts (precision accuracy), there is no perfect reflection, no reflection that, because it captures so much, so well, that it outshines all other possible reflections. Instead, an effective reflection is a genuine effort to demonstrate understanding and, potentially, to gather more information, understand the customer's goal(s), or to influence the customer. This doesn't mean there are no "bad" reflections (e.g., content reflection is incorrect, feeling word(s) used are out of synch with the customer's expression). A "good" reflection is one with no outright errors and demonstrates the service provider's *genuine* interest in understanding the customer. Even if the customer, upon hearing the service provider's reflection says, *"No, that's not right, what I meant was...,"* the provider's reflection can be defined as at least effective in getting more information from the customer's perspective—although, if this happens repeatedly, it can indicate a problem with the provider's listening and reflecting skills.

Personal anecdote: On more than one occasion over the years, I've had a senior manager from my customer's organization push back on the skill of reflecting, saying they do understand what their subordinates (their internal customers) are saying, and they don't need to reflect. I don't dispute that the senior manager does understand, but I do point out that the subordinate has no way of being sure of their manager's understanding, and simply saying, "I understand," offers no proof. My own experience is that authoritarian leaders resist reflecting in favor of claiming almost universal understanding. Participative, empathic leaders are the opposite. They seek out customer (employee) input and reflect to ensure they've understood. While it would be satisfying to say that participative, reflective leaders are more effective than autocratic leaders, it wouldn't be true. Autocratic, authoritarian leaders can be effective (e.g., they can make their "numbers"). But they may be doing so at the cost of demoralizing, even bullying, their subordinates (their internal customers).

Reflecting and Empathy

The word "Empathy" is part of the modern lexicon. We watch the news and feel empathy toward the plight of victims of natural or man-made disasters. We want empathy from our service providers, especially if there's a problem. We want, often in vain, our elected officials to have empathy for their constituents. At the same time, empathy is seldom defined in practical terms. It seems somewhat ethereal, like a feeling as opposed to an action. The position taken here is that *reflecting is empathy in action.* Reflecting is the demonstration of empathy.

Two psychologists, Daniel Goleman, and Paul Ekman,* have identified three types of empathy:

1. *Cognitive Empathy:* The ability to see another person's perspective (but perhaps without any sympathy).

2. *Emotional Empathy:* The ability to perceive another person's emotions and literally experience the feelings of others.

3. *Compassionate Empathy:* The ability to understand the feelings and perspective of another person and the desire to provide help.

Reflecting, the way it is used and defined here, is consistent with the definition of compassionate empathy. The position taken in this material is that the reflecting skill, while not always expressed, *must be available to the provider*—then the provider can choose to reflect or not. Also, reflecting is an intellectual skill rather than an emotional one. To effectively reflect, the service provider *does not* have to share the feelings of the customer. In fact, sharing the feelings of the customer may, over the long-term, become debilitating, causing the service provider to "burn-out."

---

* Ekman, Paul & Goleman, Daniel "Knowing Your Emotions, Improving Our World," (Audio Book) More Than Sound Productions (January 1, 2007)

[125]

Responding to the Customer

To be predictably judged as responsive or highly responsive, the service provider in face-to-face communication with their customers should demonstrate the following behaviors *when presenting their response to the customer* (e.g., answering customer questions, providing direction, guidance, or a recommendation):

- **Use the behavioral skills warranted by the specific situation.** If the customer asks a simple question, give a simple answer. For example, the bank customer asks, *"What's my XYZ account balance as of today?"* the provider wouldn't ask open-ended questions or formulate a reflection, they would simply answer the question. By contrast, if the customer presents a complex narrative, multi-faceted information/question, expresses a strong feeling, or presents a goal or objective, the provider might reflect to demonstrate and ensure understanding as well as asking questions to gather more information or improve clarity.

- **Present facts, data, amounts, or numbers slowly and be prepared to repeat.** Before presenting this kind of information, the provider should ensure that the customer has something to write with or otherwise record what the provider presents. (This is easily observed in a face-to-face encounter, but over the phone, the provider should ask if the customer is ready and wait for the customer to be ready— more on phone responsiveness follows in the next section of this chapter.)

- **Be concise and complete.** Concise means that the provider should find the fewest possible words to deliver meaningful content. Complete means being thorough, leaving nothing out, but adding nothing extraneous. In some cases, providers will be giving the same information to many customers one-by-one. This is the perfect opportunity to craft the message in writing and rehearse it before the customer interaction. But care should be taken *not* to sound scripted (e.g., monotone delivery, too fast a pace).

- **Present information logically.** This may mean sequential order if the provider is describing the steps the customer can take. This may mean chronological order if the provider is describing a series of past or upcoming events. This also means providing all the elements of the information at roughly the same level of detail (instead of giving a lot of detail about one element and much less detail on another). **Note:** If the provider is describing a multi-step set of actions for the customer, offer alternative sources for the description of the steps (e.g., a website, follow-up correspondence). This can be done as a supplement to a verbal description with a chance for the customer to ask clarifying questions.

- **Avoid words and phrases that are imprecise or ambiguous.** Kinda, sorta, I think, I'm not sure but, maybe, I don't know but, etc. are all words and phrases that introduce uncertainty. If uncertainty does exist, the provider should clearly acknowledge it and, if possible, commit to taking steps to develop certainty (e.g., asking questions, doing research).

- **When making a recommendation, keep it simple.** For example, provide a brief background statement (e.g., what's led to this point), state the recommendation, make three supporting points, restate the recommendation, and call for questions.** It is during Q&A that the provider can listen, reflect, and express a persuasive response. Obviously, if the service provider has been given a significant block of time to make and support their recommendation, by their B2B customer for example, the provider can provide more detail, probably supported by documentation and visuals. Even with more time, the provider should keep their presentation as simple as possible. (Keep in mind that estimates on adult attention span—focus—vary from a low of around 20 minutes to a high of 90 minutes.)

** See the YouTube video, "Making an Effective Recommendation," on my website for an example. WWW.DavidDriskill.com

Being Responsive Over the Phone[*]

Many of the behaviors for being responsive over the phone are the same as those for face-to-face responsiveness (e.g., listening, question asking, reflecting). At the same time, there are differences, the most obvious is that there are no visual customer cues (although there are ways to engage visually that will be described). The behavioral skills described in this section can be applied to a single service provider speaking with a single customer (e.g., a CRM speaking with a B2B customer), or a Customer Service Representative (CSR) working in a contact center who speaks with many customers, one at a time, throughout the day.

Before diving into the details of responsiveness over the phone, consider these three introductory points:

1. Except for certain customers and providers (e.g., B2B, very small or highly specialized providers), for most customers and providers, gone are the days when a customer picks up the phone and gets a live person. More typically, the customer must navigate a set of menu prompts. This was discussed in detail in Chapter 3 and briefly in Chapter 4, so this topic will not be readdressed here, except to say that prompts should be simple, organized according to relevance to most callers, and provide a way out of the menu. If the opening menu prompts are overly complex, too long, or irrelevant to most customers, the telephone conversation that follows will begin with a negative, unresponsive customer experience.

2. Since scripting is regrettably a standard practice for CSRs in contact centers, a brief note about scripting for contact center CSRs is worth inserting here. On the one hand, scripting the CSR will ensure uniformity, providing every customer as the call begins with what is judged as a polite greeting. On the other hand, many customers, perhaps most, are very familiar with calling a provider's contact center and they may be

---

[*] Much of what follows in this section on telephone responsiveness reflects the content of a booklet, CD, and trainer's guide I wrote in the early 2000s. Driskill, D. P. "You Are the Voice of Your Company: Superior Client Service for Financial Institutions," (2006) Human Resource Development Press, Amherst, MA

equally familiar with the script and thus, it may be perceived as lacking genuineness, much less empathy. Two examples:

- Call many providers' call center and the customer is greeted with, *"Thank you for calling the Acme Company,"* usually followed by an offer of assistance. While some experts may disagree, the position taken here is that this is clearly scripted and not natural speech. (An alternative will be provided later.)

- A second example of scripting occurs when, no matter what the customer says, the CSR says, *"I can help you with that."* The first time a customer hears this phrase, it is likely to be a positive experience. However, hearing this phrase repeatedly, especially when it turns out some CSRs can't deliver the service sought, the phrase becomes a source of irritation (at best). As with many scripted phrases, the intent is positive. But, as the phrase is used automatically with every customer, on every call, it can rightly be labeled and experienced as unresponsive.

> I can imagine a customer saying, *"I think the world is ending. I'd like you to close out my account and have my money converted to gold and sent to me via FedEx."* The CSR's scripted reply: *I can help you with that.*

3. Also note that many of the following examples of telephone responsiveness are directed at CSRs working in high-volume provider contact centers. CRMs, health professionals, lawyers, financial planners, and other providers or provider representatives may have established relationships with the customers calling in or being called. These relationships may even have evolved over months, years, and even decades into personal friendships. The principles and specific behaviors that follow still apply, but there may be additional nuances to the call. For example, a years or decades long relationship between a financial planner and their client may have evolved into a personal friendship, thus, the inbound or outbound call might include talking about family, goals, worries, and other personally relevant information. However, both parties to this relationship need to exercise care to ensure that the personal

friendship doesn't pose a barrier to the professional relationship. Both the provider and the customer *need to be able to be
unhesitatingly direct and honest with one another*, sometimes
delivering or receiving bad news—without posing a threat to
either the personal or the professional relationship.

Responsive Call Essentials: The Greeting, Holds, Transfers, Closing the Call, and Using Voice Mail

The Greeting: While every part of the customer service call is
important, how a service call begins *may* predict the quality of the
entire call. A call that begins well sets the stage for further success as
the call proceeds by setting positive tone and establishing a civil dialogue. A call that begins poorly because the service provider or CSR
is, for example, abrupt, impolite, or rushed can also set the tone for
what follows, but not in a good way. Further, customer satisfaction
with a call is not purely a function of the end result of the call. Customer satisfaction or dissatisfaction begins as they dial the phone
and proceeds minute-by-minute, even second-by-second thereafter.

An effective greeting re-identifies the provider company (since its
name was probably provided before the menu prompts), the service
person (e.g., CSR), and an offer of assistance. Thus:

Acme Health Care, this is Rachel Ward speaking, may I help you?

There may be debate about whether the CSR, in this example, should
use her full name in the greeting. While it will not be asserted here
that the use of the CSR's full name is right and first name only is
wrong, it is worth suggesting that a customer greeted with the full
name of the CSR may be more likely to perceive the CSR as a professional, versus clerical level or front-line staff. For personal security
reasons, some CSRs may be reluctant to give out their name and
instead use a pseudonym. This can work, but it requires that everyone in the service unit knows the CSR's work name.

It is also during the greeting that the pace of the call is established.
CSRs, or any provider answering or making customer calls, should
think about a moderate pace as sending out a kind of behavioral echo
to the customer. By contrast, a fast greeting that might send a message
to the customer to speed up, may be perceived as unresponsive
behavior.

Handling Holds: *No customer calls their provider to be put on hold.* Thus, while holds may be inevitable, if possible, they should be avoided. If a hold is necessary, an effective provider may use phrases that are polite and professional, as follows (for example):

- *"Are you able to hold?"*
- *"Are you able to hold while I (e.g., look up your account, research your question)?"*
- *"I need to (action), are you able to hold?"*
- *"Are you able to hold? It may take me up to 3 to 5 minutes to get back to you."*
- *"Are you able to hold while I (action)? Or would you prefer a call back?"*

Unresponsive phrases to avoid (examples):

- *"Just hold on."*
- *"You're just going to have to hold."*
- *"Can you hold for a second?"*
- *"Please ho---."*

Some call center managers will disagree with the responsiveness example used above. They don't want to ask if the customer is able to hold and they certainly don't want to offer a call back. Their reasons are focused on call center productivity and efficiency. And if their goal is to provide adequate service, they may be right. However, the goal here is to describe responsive, even superior, telephone customer service, to sound different than the typical call center, and to make that difference positive.

Transfers: *No customer calls their provider to be transferred.* Every effort should be made to avoid transfers. One way to accomplish this is by offering well-defined prompts before the call begins. For example, "If you want to X, press 1, for Y, press 2," and so on and at the same time keeping the pre-call prompts as short as possible—this is a hard task, requiring considerable effort. If a transfer must be made, a responsive format is:

- *"In order to address your question/concern, I need to transfer you to an expert. I'll stay on the line with you,"* (makes transfer), *"Mr. Jones, I have Jim Dowling on the phone. Jim, Mr. Jones*

[131]

wants to... Can you help?" (**Note:** This is a "warm" transfer. It may also be wise to get the customer's phone number in case there is a disconnect.)

In some cases, a warm transfer may not be possible. It may even be against policy in some call centers. In that event:

- *"In order to address your question/concern, I need to transfer you to an expert. Are you able to hold? It may take 3 to 5 minutes to make the connection."* (**Note:** The CSR, if allowed, may offer their extension in case the call is dropped, or if the customer wants to call back and speak with the same CSR.)

In no instance should the transfer be handled with the following or similar phrases:

- *"You'll just have to hold while I transfer your call."*

- *"I have to transfer you, hold on."*

- *"I can't help you. Hold, while I transfer you to our priority area. They should be able to help."*

> Customers typically don't want to repeat their question or concern to several different people on the same call. If they must do so, it is likely to be judged as non-responsive, even very irritating. A "warm" transfer handles this problem. It also gives the initial CSR a chance to fully reflect an understanding of the customer's inquiry or concern. Finally, it gives the customer a sense of being personally served. This is part of responsiveness.

Closing the Call: After a complex call or a call in which a commitment was made, a responsive call closing can begin with a *brief* reflection of what has happened and will happen, being specific in terms of facts and numbers. After a relatively simple call:

- *"Have I answered all your questions about X?"*

- *"Is there anything else I can help you with today?"* (If not, move on. If yes, address it.)

- *"It was a pleasure speaking with you. If you need anything else, don't hesitate to call, and thank you."*

Voice Mail: The content of an outbound message is typically well understood and won't be detailed here, except to make two points. First, if pressing 0 for immediate attention is available, it should be part of the outbound message. Second, if the provider has a time reference in the outbound message, it must be kept current. For example, if the provider will be away from X to Y dates, the message should be changed immediately after "Y" date. Or, if the providers are only available at certain times or on certain days, and that changes, the outbound message must likewise change—*immediately*.

Leaving an effective, responsive message can be a challenge. Providers may be tempted to "wing it." Don't. Especially when leaving a complex message, or a message that includes numbers or instruction, an effective message requires preparation, even a rehearsal. The message should include:

- Identification of self and company
- Purpose of the call/message
- Clear concise content (e.g., response to customer questions, instructions/guidance)
- Restatement of critical points/numbers
- Offer of follow-up access

Note: Consider using the "bookend" approach which means stating contact information at the beginning and the end of the call.

Also, service providers leaving a voice mail should consider:

- Making notes to prepare for a complex message
- Say and repeat numbers slowly (putting a "beat" between each number)
- Eliminate nonsense sounds/words (e.g., er, uhm, kinda, like, sorta)
- DO NOT leave transaction-specific or personally identifying numbers (e.g., Social Security number)

Handling Challenging Calls Responsively

Anyone handling inbound or outbound customer calls, whether as an individual service provider or as a CSR in a contact center, will experience challenging calls. These are calls that can't be handled quickly and easily and will often include an emotional or very emotional

[133]

customer (e.g., an unreasonable demand, an angry customer, a confused customer). The following provides some examples of challenging calls and some service provider responses—some good, some bad.

Challenging Call—Customer says, *"I want to speak with your manager!"* (Either as the call begins or having been told something they did not want to hear.)

Possible types of responses:

- *"Before I transfer you, I'd like to try to help."*
- *"In order to transfer you to the right person, I'll need some background information."* (Client provides background.) *"If you'll let me, that's something I can help you with."*
- *"My manager is not immediately available, but I'll be glad to give them the specific information they need to call you back."*

Responses to avoid:

- *"I'll transfer you, but that won't change the answer you get."*
- *"I'm not sure who to transfer you to until you calm down and explain the situation."*

Obviously, if the system and policy allow for it and the customer continues to insist on speaking with a manager, make a warm transfer (described earlier).

Challenging Call—Customer says, *"Can't you make an exception...?"*

Possible responses:

- *"Sir, we've passed the legal deadline (e.g., IRS rule, transaction processing deadline) and we're not able to exercise any discretion in the case of a regulatory requirement."*
- *"I've reviewed your request with my manager, and we don't make an exception in these situations. Let's talk about what we can do."*

Responses to avoid:

- *"If it were up to me, I'd make an exception, but my hands are tied."*
- *"I'm just following the rules."*
- *"The policy makes no sense to me either, but I have no choice."*

Challenging Call—Customer says, *"I'm so mad and frustrated..."*

Possible responses:

- *"Help me understand your perspective about what's happened so far that makes you mad and frustrated."* (Provider listens and reflects fully. The problem may still be present, but at least the customer feels that someone has listened.)
- *"You want* (customer goal), *but what's happened is* (customer perspective). *Here is what I'd like to propose* (the action the service provider can take).

(**Note:** There will be more detail on the topic of handling challenging calls and problems in the next chapter on Problem Recovery.)

Responses to avoid:

- *"Don't feel that way. You've got to calm down if you want me to help you."*
- *"There's no reason to be mad at me."*
- *"I understand exactly how you feel, but..."*

Challenging Call—Customer says: *"I'm confused. I'm not following any of this."* (The customer may communicate this message via tone versus words.)

Possible responses:

- *"This can be complicated. I'm happy to answer your questions, go back over the entire process, or both."*
- Slow the pace.
- Repeat the big picture or the overall goal.
- Present action in sequential order (giving the customer the time to make notes).

Responses to avoid:

- *"It's really simple. Anyone can understand."*
- *"I've never had a problem explaining this to anyone else."*

> **Note:** A simple web search on best practices will yield a true plethora of information about conference calls and video conferencing. No effort will be made to reflect all that information here. Instead, I've focused on those practices most relevant to WACW and practices in which I've seen repeated service failures. These failures, often in the simplest aspects of the call, can also be defined as unresponsive, since the customer didn't get everything they wanted.

Visualizing the Customer on a Phone Call

As stated earlier, the fundamental difference between face-to-face communication and communicating with customers over the phone is the lack of visual information. There are at least three ways to address this:

1. If the provider has met the customer in person on one or more occasion, visualizing may not be too difficult. During the call, the provider can visualize the customer in relation to the content of the call and how their facial expression might change as the call proceeds.

2. The provider (e.g., CSR) can simply try to visualize a customer they've never met. Is the customer young or older, smiling or frowning, nodding, or shaking their head? Much of the visualization will come from the customer's verbal mannerisms (e.g., tone, pace). This is an imperfect approach, but it can fill in at least part of the visual gap.

3. The provider can be looking at an array of simple drawings or photos of customers showing a variety of facial expressions. (**Personal Note:** I've seen this to be very effective in large volume call centers. Simple drawings were used showing smiling, frowning, confused, sad, happy faces, etc.)

Responsive Conference Calls and Video Conferencing

Every skill and best practice for face-to-face and telephone responsiveness carries forward—with the appropriate flexibility—to being responsive in the service provider's management of conference calls and video conferencing. (e.g., question asking, reflecting, verbal mannerisms). That said, there are some unique attributes, and thus distinct best practices, for both conference calls and video conferences.

Since the preceding and following material is focused on responsiveness as an element of WACW, the following information is intended as a guide for service providers having a conference call or video conference with their customer. The following ideas and information are generally targeted at the B2B service provider communicating with their B2B customer. Most of what follows can also be applied to one-on-one video and conference calls.

B2B Conference Calls—Some Best Practices

- Involve the customer in agenda planning/creation.
- Test the technology before every call.
- The service provider should be on the call, ready to begin, at least 5 to 10 minutes before the call.
- All calls *must* have a Chair—*focused on managing the call vs. meeting content.*
- Have an agenda with timing for each item.
- Someone must record decisions and action items from the call. Ideally, this person has no vested interest in the content of the call.[*]
- The chair reflects to conclude each agenda item and to selectively demonstrate understanding of customer input, concerns, and problems.
- Warn speakers as their time is running out.
- Use a normal tone, don't shout, and ensure that the speaker is close to the microphone.
- Avoid extraneous noise (papers, key clacks, tapping). Mute out unless you are speaking.
- Don't say anything in the room that you don't want everyone to hear.
- Presenters guide participants through materials via slide numbers.
- If slides are used, don't read every sentence—summarize and pause to let people digest the content.

---

[*] Meeting minutes are often taken, reflecting everything discussed. If regulation or policy requires detailed minutes, so be it. However, meeting notes, focused on decisions made and action to be taken (by whom and when), may be more meaningful and useful.

- Recognize (and possibly announce) that conference calls are not secure.

- *Always* end on time or early.

Video Conferencing

- Apply all the best practices from conference calls.

- When more than three sites are involved, audio only may be the "better" choice.

- Keep video-projected support materials very simple. You should be able to read the words on a piece of paper from 4 to 5 feet away before using it on screen.

- Dress simply for the call. Avoid patterns; they may create a video halo.

- As a participant, raise your hand (slowly) before you interject a comment, or raise your hand electronically, if the technology allows.

- Rely less on body language or facial expression than in a face-to-face interaction. (Be careful to avoid a strong facial expression as a mute reaction to someone's presentation.)

- Look at the camera when you speak, not your own image on the screen.

- Be aware that video conference microphones in a dedicated video meeting room may be more sensitive than a speakerphone or even a conference call microphone—be careful about what you say—even though you are off camera, you can still be heard.

- If you need to ask a question, make sure your image is on the monitor before you begin.

- Try to present ideas, recommendations, or content in "threes"—three points, three topics, three things to remember. People will tend to remember three goals, ideas, facts, etc.

Additional Notes about Conference Calls and Video Conferencing

1. Perhaps surprisingly, it is recommended here that the service provider use the reflecting skill more sparingly during a conference call or video conference than during a face-to-face meeting or one-on-one phone call. Reflecting should be used to segue from one agenda item to the next, or to demonstrate understanding of a problem expressed during the call or video. Reflecting more frequently will be experienced as tedious and unhelpful by some participants as well as lengthening the interaction.

2. Before the pandemic, the duration of video or conference calls typically ran from a low of 15 minutes to a high of 1 hour. With the pandemic, the length and frequency of both kinds of customer communication has gone up. At the same time, the demands on attention span during a conference call or video conference are greater, more concentrated than during a one-on-one call or a face-to-face interaction. Beware of "Zoom Fatigue."[**] It is suggested here that shorter and more frequent meetings may be more effective than fewer, but longer meetings. However, it must be acknowledged that the pandemic has forced almost everyone to adapt to "the new normal."[*]

Responsive Email, Text, Chat, etc.

Email

The first iteration of what would become email goes back decades as a tool for academics to share files and messages. Forward to the present day, and email is ubiquitous. Service providers, large and small, use email to communicate with customers and, in turn, customers with their providers. Interestingly, with the advent of texting, chat, and other computer mediated communication channels, email may become as antiquated as sending a handwritten letter via the postal service. But not yet. At least for the next few years, it's reasonable to

---

[**] "How To Combat Zoom Fatigue," Fosslien & Duffy, Harvard Business Review—Analytic Services, April 29, 2020.

[*] Virtual Work Meetings During the COVID-19 Pandemic: The Good, Bad, and Ugly Katherine A. Karl, Joy V. Peluchette, and Navid Aghakhani (2021) SAGE

predict that email remains one of the primary communication channels and an integral tool for responsiveness to all kinds of customers,
both internal and external.

So, what constitutes a responsive versus a non-responsive email?
More specifically, what are the practical best practices that will, if
applied, tend to produce an email that the customer judges as being
responsive?

Three overarching points about email:

1. Not all emails are created equal. It would be easy, and perhaps
    politically correct, to say that every email is just as important as
    every other email; that every email should be given the same level
    of attention and effort as every other email. However, it's not true.
    Some emails are more important than others. For example, an
    email to an external customer providing a complex response to an
    inquiry can be judged as more important than an email to a col-
    league answering a simple process inquiry. Yes, in both cases
    basic email etiquette (civility) should be employed, but the cus-
    tomer response will and should get greater attention and effort
    than the collegial response. (It should be acknowledged that mis-
    judgment about the relative importance of an email is inevitable,
    but judging importance is still important for efficiency and the
    appropriate expenditure of energy.)

2. Email creates a permanent electronic record, and no email system
    is entirely secure. Every email has the chance to be read by any-
    one, at any time, with any agenda. Every email has the chance to
    be used in the assignment of liability to individuals and organiza-
    tions. *Every email has the chance to be reprinted on page 1 of the
    New York Times.* As a result of these realities, care should be taken
    about what to include or not include in an email. Exclude any
    inappropriate language. Exclude gossip. Exclude personal identifi-
    cation information (e.g., Social Security number). Exclude expres-
    sion of culpability unless approved by legal counsel. Be aware
    that we are increasingly in a recorded environment in a litigious
    culture. (In some circumstances, service providers may well be
    better off with a private face-to-face encounter.)

3. This third note is the most important. If the service provider is
    writing a particularly important or sensitive email, it's wise to
    draft it and not send it. Instead, walk away for an hour or two.

When the service provider returns to the email, it is almost certain that revisions will be made that improve the email. The point here is one that is commonly understood by most effective writers; *the key to good writing is editing.*

Additional Email Best Practices for Responsiveness

- Read it before hitting "send."
- Address the email *only* after all editing is complete.
- Consider not completing the subject line until all editing is complete.
- One topic per one email (more than one topic can get lost).[*]
- The provider needs to know the preferences of their customer—do they want more information, or less (default to less).
- Opening sentence, short paragraph or list, and closing—that's enough.
- Use bulleted lists of sentence fragments (for brevity/clarity).
- Use the subject line to inform ("FYI" does not inform).
- Use a polite opening and respectful language to add positive tone to emails.
- Greet a group with "Hello" and an individual with their name.
- **Do not** use "Reply All" unless necessary (be careful of listserv, in which emails are automatically distributed to a mailing list).
- Always ask, "Is this email necessary?" (Many are not.) Would a phone call be better?
- Set up an alert if a critical email is expected.
- Don't **ever** send an angry or sarcastic email.
- Don't join an email chain (3 or more emails); pick up the phone.
- Let email do its work—don't call right after sending.

---

[*] There are exceptions. If you originate or participate in email communication requiring a "chain of evidence" (e.g., other emails, documents, records), completeness may be more important than brevity.

[141]

Chat, Instant Messaging, and Texting

There are several differences between email when compared to chat, instant messaging (IM), and texting. Two differences, especially relevant to chat and IM, are immediacy and brevity.

1. **Immediacy:** The customer's expectation when using chat or IM is for an almost immediate response. In contrast, when the customer emails or even texts the service provider, a delay in the response will not necessarily be judged as non-responsive, unless the delay is significant (e.g., longer than the norm). As the labels "Chat" and "Instant" imply, the dialogue between customer and provider should be happening in almost real-time. For the responsive service provider, immediacy requires coverage at all times. Chat or IM are offered as a channel of communication.

2. **Brevity:** IM and Chat inquiries will tend to be short, reflecting a single question or concern. Likewise, the service provider's response. It will be short and to the point. And there may be a bit of real-time back and forth between the customer and the provider. (If the back and forth becomes excessive, the service provider is well advised to pick up the phone.) Also, some of the etiquette associated with an email (e.g., greeting, polite closing) may be absent from IM and Chat. Abbreviations, sentence fragments, and acronyms may also be more frequently used in Chat and IM versus email.

Selected Best Practices for Chat and IM

- While brief, Chat *can* include an opening and a closing—"Hello" and "Thank you."
- Check the status of the recipient (e.g., internal/external customer), if available. If they're "away" or "busy," use another channel (e.g., email) or wait.
- Don't deliver bad or negative news via Chat or IM.
- As with all communication, only use abbreviations and acronyms known by the recipient.
- If offering the Chat feature to customers, the provider must ensure 100% coverage during the times specified.

- Just as over the phone (mentioned earlier), avoid scripting Chat responses or inquiries. (Although Chat may begin with a selection of frequently asked questions.)

- As a Chat/IM provider, customer input is also gathering. Examining the records may highlight customer themes, both good and problematic, and opportunities.

- Chat/IM can include sentence fragments and *short* lists, as opposed to longer narrative.

Selected Best Practices for Texting

- Texting is the province of mobile devices. This may not be an appropriate communications channel between service providers and their external customers.

- Beware of autocorrect—read it before sending.

- Be concise, but more information can be provided in a text than via Chat or IM.

- Providers should think twice about emojis, *then bias toward **not** using them*, especially with external customers or unknown recipients. (It's annoying and the sender may be taken less seriously.)

- Don't text sensitive or negative information; pick up the phone, have a face-to-face meeting.

- Don't text during situations requiring your full attention (e.g., in a meeting with customers, while driving, during a conversation with a colleague—an internal customer).

NOTE: SMS (Short Message Service) and texting are almost indistinguishable. Texting allows for longer messages and graphics (emojis), while SMS doesn't.

An additional note about Texting and SMS: It is recommended here that Texting and SMS *not* be a primary channel of communication between service providers and their customers, especially between B2B providers and their B2B customers. By their very nature, Texting and SMS are somewhat informal communication channels. Email, face-to-face, and telephone conversations are more formal (*not* unfriendly) and give both the provider and the customer communication channels that allow for a more complete and more responsive interaction. However, it is also understood that the pandemic has

[143]

changed the way we interact. Even when the pandemic ends (becoming endemic), some channels of communication providers may have used in the short term may persist over the long term. There is no perfect answer here except to say that service provider communication should, no matter the channel, be thoughtful and highly disciplined.

A Note about Chatbots: A chatbot is simply technology used to simulate a human being in response to a customer inquiry or input. Chatbots have been around since the mid '60s and are now part of the tech landscape (think HAL from 2001 A Space Odyssey; think Alexa on your kitchen table). The benefits of chatbots are ease and speed of access, usefulness for responding to simple inquiries, and endless patience. The downside is the inability, at present, of a chatbot to deal with highly complex or novel interactions. As stated earlier, while the term *artificial intelligence* is in wide use, at present, chatbots are limited by their underlying trigger words and algorithms. Chatbots are becoming more capable and are in wider use. It's not hard to predict continued, even exponential growth, in the coming years. Chatbots will increasingly become part of the mosaic of service provider responsiveness. (ChatGPT seems to be the next step in technology interacting in a "natural" conversational manner.)

Responsiveness In Relation to the Other Elements of What All Customers Want (WACW)

1. If the provider *is* behaviorally responsive but fails to deliver one or more of the other elements of WACW (e.g., Timely, Accurate), the service interaction is likely to produce customer dissatisfaction.

2. If the provider effectively delivers on all the elements of WACW but fails to be behaviorally responsive (e.g., fails to listen), the service interaction is likely to produce dissatisfaction.

3. If the provider is behaviorally unresponsive *and* fails to deliver on one or more of the other elements of WACW, the service interaction is likely to produce dissatisfaction and, potentially, extreme dissatisfaction.

4. If the provider is behaviorally responsive and effectively delivers all the other elements of WACW, the service interaction is likely to produce satisfaction and, potentially, extreme, and recurring satisfaction, even "delight."

Responsiveness in Relation to Various Customer Behaviors

In each of the preceding chapters covering the other elements of WACW (e.g., Accuracy, Timeliness), the chapter concluded with the application of the element to different kinds of internal and external customers. This chapter takes a different approach, reflecting the difference between responsiveness and the other elements of WACW. Responsiveness is different in the sense that how the service provider responds to their customer is driven less by the type of customer and more by the provider's behavior. (And it must always be remembered that *everyone is a customer*.) What follows is a list of a few common customer behaviors paired with a provider response that can be judged as responsive.

The customer and provider behaviors on the following page are representational. A list of all possible interactions would be virtually endless, especially considering the nuances of body language and verbal mannerisms combined with verbal content. However, the content that follows can be useful as a starting point for thinking about actual customer behaviors and how the provider might formulate a responsive reply, question, or reflection.

Customer Behavior	Provider Response/Behavior
Provides specific numbers or names (e.g., address, dollar amount).	Reflects verbatim.
Asks a brief, simple, and face-based question with no exceptional verbal manner or body language cues.	Answers the question. (No need for a reflection or question.)
Asks a brief, simple, and fact-based question with significant verbal manner or body language cues (e.g., indicating concern, worry).	Answers the question. Provider may ask, *"Are there other concerns I can help you with?"* (Open-ended/Reflective question)
Presents a narrative which includes both their experience and goal(s).	Uses an interchangeable or summary reflection to capture narrative. Reflects the customer's goal(s).
Presents a fairly long narrative. No strong emotion expressed.	Summary reflection.
Presents a strong emotion (e.g., frustration, worry) along with narrative content that explains the emotion (at least in the view of the customer).	Reflects feeling and content (e.g., *"You feel* (feeling word) *because* (content)*"*. **NOTE: Handling the emotional customer (e.g., angry), is addressed more thoroughly in the next chapter on Effective Problem Recovery.**
Customer presents goal(s), but they are not well defined/explained. Customer may use words that lack precision (e.g., "kinda," "sorta," "I'm not sure, but…").	Uses a mix of direct, open-ended, and perhaps forced choice direct questions to clarify/articulate the customer's goal(s). This interaction may go back and forth for some time before mutual understanding is achieved.
Customer presents goal(s) supported by narrative content, but goals or content are not entirely clear.	Based on experience or on an extended dialogue, the provider presents an additive/interpretative reflection. (The provider, e.g., a CSR, may have extensive experience with similar customers enabling an additive reflection.)

A Call to Action

Applying WACW to a real-world situation is the best way to understand it. Applying responsiveness to a real-world situation can be achieved by using the various best practices from this chapter that attach to specific activities (e.g., running a conference call or video conference, reviewing an email).

What follows is a specific example of one application of responsiveness as part of WACW The checklist that follows is designed to reinforce responsive behaviors for CRSs working in a large volume contact center. The behavioral checklist below is designed to help supervisors and other monitors review CSR behavior handling inbound calls from customers. The results of the checklist can then be used to provide feedback to CSRs. The example provided here to how responsive behavior can be described, assessed, and then used to guide feedback.

> **Personal Note:** Early in my consulting career, I was asked by one of my customers to find a way to monitor and measure the quality of the interaction between CSRs and external customers calling for service. My customer was a large investment management firm and a pioneer in using 800 number priority access to its financial service customers. The behavioral checklist that came out of this assignment was one of the first of its kind and has been revised and updated many times in the intervening years. The partial example provided on the next few pages reflects that work and some subsequent improvements.

Standard/Responsive Behavior

	Yes	No	N/A
GREETING/INITIATING			
• ID "Company/Dept."			
• Self ID (Last name if policy allows)			
• Offer Assistance/State Purpose			
• Timely Greeting			
QUESTION ASKING			
• Questions Relevant and Complete			
• Asks Direct Questions			
• ID Caller before Relating Account Information			
PROVIDING INFORMATION			
• Reflects Understanding			
• Reflects Customer Feeling and Verbal Content (if appropriate)			
• Provides Accurate Information and/or Data (e.g., numbers)			
• Provides Complete/Detailed Information			
• Repeats Key Points to Clarify			
• Explains Delays/Avoids "Dead Air"			
HOLDS/WAITS			
• Request Client Agreement			
• Long Hold—Offers Callback			
• Thanks the Customer for Waiting			

Continued →

	Yes	No	N/A
TRANSFERS			
• Offers Direct Assistance (If able—to avoid transfer)			
• Offers Voice Mail			
• Ensures Connection			
• Announce Call and Reason ("Warm Transfer")			
CLOSING			
• Action Summary (e.g., CSR has done, will do, customer action)			
• Assess Satisfaction/Agreement			
• Give Name for Callback (If warranted and if policy permits)			
• Offer Further (Future) Assistance			
• Thanks Caller/Polite Closing Remark			

Above Standard Behaviors—Highly Responsive

	Check
• Reverses a Negative Call into Positive through Behavioral Skills (e.g., reflects understanding of Customer Feeling and Source)	
• Identifies a Problem Outside of Call and Resolves (goes beyond the caller's request)	
• Uses Additive/Interpretive Reflection to Clarify Customer Goal(s)	
• Anticipates Problem/Takes Steps to Prevent Future Problems	
• Demonstrates Exemplary Technical Knowledge	
• Other (describe)	

Below Standard Behaviors—Unresponsive

	Check
• Disclosed confidential Information or Data to Client	
• Assigns Blame for Problem(s) to Another Person or Area	
• Provides Inaccurate Information	
• Provides Information/Data to Customer that is *Not* Timely	
• Provides Information/Data to Customer that is *Not* Useful (e.g., missing action steps)	
• Rude or Confrontational with Customer	
• Other (describe)	

Checklists of any kind have both value and limitations:

- The inherent limitation of a checklist, and especially a behavioral checklist, is that it can't capture all the possible nuances of a call between a service provider and their customer. In fact, in the hands of an inexperienced or unqualified call monitor, a call judged as successful and responsive can, from the customer's perspective, be a total failure. Likewise, a call judged as non-responsive according to the "rules" of the checklist, can be exactly what the customer both wanted and needed.

- The value of a behavioral checklist is that it provides a kind of baseline for a call between a service provider and their customer. It ensures that key features of responsiveness are included in every call. It is an ironic reality that often senior, highly experienced professionals make simple but extremely serious mistakes.[*] A behavioral checklist, along with effective training, on-the-job support, and feedback from a qualified professional can be an integral and vital ingredient for responsive, even superior customer service.

Now, on to the final element of WACW, Effective Problem Recovery.

---

[*] Gawande, Atul "The Checklist Manifesto: How to Get Things Right" (2010) Metropolitan Books, Henry Holt and Company, New York.

The best laid plans of mice and men often go awry.

—Robert burns

Richard: *"He's here. He'll get no satisfaction out of us. Don't let him see you beg. Take it like a man!"*

Geoffrey: *"You fool! As if the way one falls down matters!"*

Richard: *"Well, when the fall is all that's left, it matters a great deal."*

—The Lion in Winter
(1968)

Chapter 7
Problem Recovery

*A customer is anyone in a position to feel satisfied or
dissatisfied about **problem recovery** and can act based
on their satisfaction or dissatisfaction.*

Problems are inevitable. Mistakes will be made. Service will be late. Access will be denied. Usefulness will be lacking. People will be unresponsive. If it can go wrong, at some point it will go wrong. These are among the facts of life and, more specifically, the facts of customer service.

Interestingly, and perhaps predictably, service providers have gotten markedly better at problem recovery over the past couple of decades. In years past, *"Do you have a receipt?", "I can't help you with that,"* or *"You'll have to call back"* were typical responses to a customer with a service problem. Over the past couple of decades, many service providers have set up problem recovery processes that make it easier for the customer. For example, if a customer has a service problem with Amazon, almost no questions are asked, and the customer is provided with an easy-to-use RMA (Returned Merchandize Authorization) label. (Unfortunately for the environment, the returned merchandise may be disposed of because the cost of restocking is greater than the return for doing so, although a returned goods auction business is beginning to emerge.)

With all the improvements, there are often still issues with problem recovery. The recovery process may be too complex or ask too much from the customer. Individual providers may become defensive or argumentative. The technology (e.g., provider website) may be poorly designed or require the input of identifying numbers or facts that are hard for the customer to locate (e.g., serial numbers, account numbers, the specific date of a transaction). Thus effective, even satisfying problem recovery, remains elusive and an unmet challenge for many service providers. This may be especially true for internal customers (e.g., employees) experiencing a problem with their provider (e.g., their supervisors). Provider organizations have typically not set up robust processes for internal problem resolution, and the typical recommendation if an employee is having a problem with another employee or supervisor is to go to Human Resources, which, in turn, may lead to real or perceived additional problems.

There are four strategically critical principles about problems and problem recovery that are important to understand as this chapter begins:

1. *Service organizations and individuals define their values, character, and culture by how they respond to problems.* As an individual, how you recover or fail to recover from problems defines you as a person.

2. *The customer's "antenna" goes up when they experience a service problem.* They are more likely to be judgmental and express strong emotions (e.g., frustration, anger, impatience) and their sense of time (duration) may be distorted (e.g., subjectively experiencing delays longer than actual clock time).

3. *Customers experiencing poor problem recovery are more likely to end their relationship with the provider and tell others about their experience—possibly many others.* In the B2B relationship, it may take longer and include multiple poor experiences, but the principle remains the same.

4. *Customers experiencing extremely effective problem recovery from their provider may experience a rise in their satisfaction, possibly higher than before the problem occurred.* Customers experiencing *superior* problem recovery (an unexpectedly positive experience) may move from being a generally satisfied customer to being a loyal customer, becoming a long-term advocate.

The Basics: Some of What Customers Want and Don't Want When a Service Problem Happens

This chapter will go into considerable detail about sources of service problems and problem recovery methods (both systemic and behavioral). At the same time, much of what the customer wants and does not want during problem recovery can be quite basic.

What the Customer Wants	What the Customer Doesn't Want
They want the problem fixed/resolved.	They don't want a new, additional problem, or for the same problem to reoccur.
They want problem recovery to be easy.	They don't want a complex, hard to follow problem recovery process.
They want problem recovery to be fast.	They don't want the problem recovery process to be slow and ponderous/bureaucratic.
They want the provider to apologize.*	They don't want the provider to blame someone else or another organization and they don't want the provider to become defensive or argumentative.
They want the provider to take accountability.	They don't want the provider to deny the problem and they don't want to be blamed for the problem.
They want the provider to take their problem seriously (no matter the magnitude).	They don't want the provider to trivialize or deny their perception of the problem.
An explicit affirmation that the problem has been resolved/fixed.	They don't want to be left uncertain/unsure (the overused word *"closure"* fits here).
Some customers, especially B2B, want in-process updates during problem recovery.	They don't want to be "left in the dark" during problem recovery.

Continued →

---

* Taking accountability for problem resolution should not be confused with assuming liability. In some provider settings, like financial, legal or insurance services, it may be unwise in the extreme to assign or assume culpability for a problem. Doing so can lead to legal action. Thus, the provider can say, "I'm sorry you have this problem and I'm going to do everything I can to resolve it," versus, "I'm sorry we made a mistake." In some cases, depending on the type of provider and service problem, the later admission might be totally appropriate, in others, ill advised. The provider organization should have clear and unambiguous policy and supportive training on this topic.

What the Customer Wants	What the Customer Doesn't Want
If they speak with a provider representative (e.g., CSR), they want that person to have the necessary authority and be polite, professional, competent, and someone who listens.	If they speak with a provider representative (e.g., CSR), they don't want that person to be impatient, incompetent, lack the necessary authority, or a person who does not listen.
If they use the provider website, they want it to be structured so that the problem can be readily identified and resolved (e.g., easy to edit, menu driven).	If they use the provider website, they don't want it to be hard/complex to navigate or require the input of the same information more than once.

Note: Many of the service problems used as examples in this and earlier chapters describe a single problem and a single preferred or discouraged response. In reality, some service problems may go on for days, weeks, even months with multiple interactions between the provider and their customer (e.g., a customer in conflict with a governmental agency, an insurance company, their bank). Long duration problem recovery will be judged by the customer based on *each contact* with the provider (e.g., via phone, email) and each incremental outcome of the problem recovery process. Every single step in the problem recovery process will be judged by every customer. Further, each contact and the overall outcome will be judged relative to provider performance in all elements of WACW.

Responding to the Emotional Customer (e.g., angry, frustrated, disappointed)

When a service problem occurs, emotions can run high for both the customer and the service provider. Effectively responding to an emotional, very angry or frustrated customer, often means that the service provider has to first manage their own emotions. After all, if someone is yelling at you and basic civility has gone out the window, it's hard to not feel attacked and become defensive. And a more senior person like a supervisor or manager telling you to, "not take it personally" is not only not helpful, but it also demonstrates a complete lack of empathy.

So, what to do? First and foremost, recognize that there is no magical word or phrase that will always reduce the customer's anger. And, no matter what, you may feel unjustly attacked. And you *do* take it personally. However, if you express defensiveness, or even worse, express anger toward the customer, the situation will almost inevitably get worse.

Some customers, some people are angry by nature. Others, most people, get angry about a particular situation—the service problem. The answer to both is to listen. Let the customer talk. The cliché that sometimes you just need to let people "vent" is often true. However, the customer may remain angry, but they may also give you the information you need to formulate a response that reflects your understanding and offers options or even solutions.

Don't go too fast or too slow. If you try to accelerate toward a solution, even if it is the right one, going too fast can quickly become yet another problem in the eyes of the customer. Responding with empathy (reflecting your understanding of the customer's experience) and identifying the actions you will take and the actions that the customer can take may ease the situation. In all cases the service provider must remain in control and losing control will only escalate an already negative situation.

Recognize that customers get angry. While hard to do without feeling attached and defensive, let them be angry—don't deny them the opportunity.

Some problems have no solution. An upset, angry, or frustrated customer is inevitable. There is no fix. There is no positive resolution. A medical patient or patient's family given news of a chronic or terminal condition can't be expected to reign in their emotions, at least not right away. The financial service customer who has sustained a large loss, even though they were repeatedly told that loss is possible, can be expected to blame the provider, at least initially. The customer who bought a product that breaks the day after the warrantee expired will not be happy, and there is often nothing the service provider can do, except listen. In these kinds of cases, the individual service provider experiencing the customer's negative emotions, often aimed directly at them, needs a support system. They need someone they can talk to about their feelings after having been yelled at or have otherwise been the target of the customer's frustration or anger. Too few service provider organizations have specific, well defined, and accessible resources for helping individual employees after they've been essentially beat up by a customer. And that's one of the reasons that burn-out among individual service personnel is almost epidemic.

Sources and Examples of Customer Service Problems

The sources and examples of customer service problems that follow reflect the three components of the organization (see Chapter 1 for more detail about each component):

1. People
2. Process
3. Technology

1. **People-based customer service problem examples in relation to each element of WACW.**

- **Accuracy:** People make mistakes. They transpose numbers making them incorrect. They set an expectation for further action or follow-up and then fail to deliver on the expectation. They make things up (e.g., facts, past events) to sound knowledgeable or to evade responsibility.

- **Timeliness:** People can be late or unavailable when they are supposed to be available. People can fail to effectively manage the customer's experience of timeliness and waiting time. People can be slow (e.g., slower than others performing the same or similar function—slower than the norm).

- **Access:** People can be inaccessible or hard/slow to access. It can be difficult to access the right person (e.g., the person with the authority to make certain decisions). People can have accents, regional dialects, or pacing that make the information they provide inaccessible.

- **Usefulness:** The person the customer reaches is unable to provide useful information or guidance (e.g., the person is untrained or inexperienced). The person serving the customer leaves out critical facts or information, disabling the customer to take the action they want.

- **Responsiveness:** The service person (e.g., CSR) doesn't listen to the customer and may claim understanding but is unable or unwilling to demonstrate it explicitly. The service person demonstrates impatience, irritation, or frustration with the customer—via tone or verbal expression.

2. **Process-based customer service problem examples in relation to each element of WACW.**

    A general note about process: Deming and Juran, preeminent researchers and process quality experts in the mid to late 20th century (see Chapter 1), both asserted that 80% or more of quality problems (e.g., errors, being late, inaccessible) are the result of flawed process. Service problems are literally "baked" into the work process. This is illustrated by the Pareto Principle, or the 80/20 rule, which asserts that 20% of actions (steps in the process) will account for 80% of outcomes (e.g., service problems)—also referred to as the "law of the vital few." The vital few in this case is the 20% of process flaws leading to 80% of process-based customer service problems. Problematic processes can be addressed via continuing process analysis leading to process improvement, or even process reengineering.

    - **Accuracy:** The process designed to produce an accurate outcome (e.g., number, fact) is missing, randomly eliminates, or inserts one variable making the outcome always or randomly incorrect. This problem is likely the result of a missing or inadequate process control step, the process control step not being implemented, or an *ad hoc* process work-around.

    - **Timeliness:** A strategically important or B2B customer needs something (e.g., a report, an action, research) almost immediately (e.g., *"I need it yesterday!"*). The Service Level Agreement (SLA) with the client sets the timeliness standard for this process at 24 to 36 hours. A decision needs to be made to either put aside the SLA or dissatisfy a strategically important individual or B2B customer. In either case, the process failed to incorporate exceptional circumstances as a timeliness standard.

    - **Access:** Before gaining access, the customer is forced by the provider's process to fill out the same questionnaire each time a certain request is made, or an appointment scheduled. The process does not incorporate saving the customer's information and only asking for confirmation of continued validity or edits to the questionnaire because of changes on the customer's side. (**Personal Note:** I've noticed this process/access flaw repeatedly in dealing with both government agencies and healthcare providers.)

- **Usefulness:** The customer asks for "X" (e.g., information, guidance) and is given "Y," where "Y" is useless or less useful than "X." Usefulness of the process can also be viewed relative to the proportionality of the provider's response. For example, a serious mistake is made, costing the customer time and considerable frustration, and the provider gives the customer a five-dollar gift certificate. The process that led to the gift certificate being issued is, in this example, wildly disproportionate and not only useless but also insulting. (This can also be used as an example of one problem leading to another as well as processing unresponsiveness.)

- **Responsiveness:** The customer (in this example a patient of a healthcare provider) has a serious, but not life-threatening problem, calls for an appointment, is kept on hold for 20+ minutes, and then asked to use the provider's website. The patient goes to the website and finds that no appointments are available for more than 30 days. The patient, in pain, either waits the 30 days or is forced to exaggerate their symptoms to be seen sooner or go to the ER. In either case, the process is unresponsive.

3. **Technology-based customer service problem examples in relation to each element of WACW.**

   - **Accuracy:** While technology in all its forms has reduced errors overall when compared to manual processes, it can also be a source of error. For example, in batch processing[*], if an error occurs, the technology involved will automatically multiply the error. For another highly specific example, in the 2000 U.S.

---

[*] Batch processing is a computer process in which tasks for identical activities are grouped and processed together (e.g., credit card billing statements). Thus, instead of generating a bill, for example, on a customer-by-customer basis, all bills are processed together as a batch.

presidential election, Florida ballets were partially/incompletely punched, leading to "hanging chads" which, in turn, led to an unusually high number of votes being judged as invalid.

- **Timeliness:** Like accuracy, the application of technology to the customer service delivery process has sped up that process, especially when compared to manual service delivery. But technology can also make service delivery less timely than desired or expected by the customer. For example, if the customer wants to speak with a live person by phone, they will often have to go through one or more menus before they can do so. And often, having gone through the menus, the customer has to wait on hold before finally getting to a person who *may* be able to help.

- **Access:** A poorly designed website, hard to navigate or not organized to reflect the hierarchy of what customers want, are all examples of technology as a barrier to customer access. Similarly, call center technology that makes the customer wade through multiple menus or asks for account or other numbers that the customer may or may not have on hand, all contribute to a barrier to access and thus a service problem.

- **Usefulness:** Like access, a poorly designed website, hard to navigate or not organized to reflect the hierarchy of what customers want, all diminish the usefulness of the technology. Customers want technology to be easy to use the first time they use it *and* the 20th time they use it. And that's often a service problem in relation to usefulness. Designing a technology interface effectively for the customer's first use may be ineffective for repeat users. Thus, to be useful, such technology must offer the repeat customer a way to shorten their journey to quickly get to what they want.

- **Responsiveness:** Technology responsiveness is, at least in part, the foregoing elements of WACW. Thus, responsive technology is accurate, timely, accessible, and useful. A service failure in one or more than one element of WACW creates a responsiveness service problem. Moving forward into the not-too-distant future, voice response technology like Siri and Alexa can be expected to evolve (see the discussion of Chatbots in Chapter 6). But even now, customers may judge such technology as responsive or unresponsive depending on performance (e.g., provides the information or assistance needed, or does so only after repeated attempts, or fails to do so entirely).

Effective Problem Recovery

The list of "Dos and Don'ts" provided early in this chapter can be used to both assess current problem recovery strategies and to communicate basic priorities to service provider personnel. The following goes into more detail.

If a service provider was able to design an effective and complete approach to problem recovery beginning with a blank sheet of paper, it would comprise each element of the organization. But the order of design would be different than that presented previously. Instead of People, Process, and Technology, the design of a complete and predictably effective and successful problem recovery system would comprise, in the order of its design, Process, Technology, and People.

1. Process

Problem recovery begins with the design of the problem recovery process. Which, in turn, would begin by identifying all possible service problems in detail. Then the provider would deploy process design experts to construct a process for each service problem, which may include, but not be restricted to:

- Outline process scope (boundaries)
- Identify/define process inputs and outputs
- Develop process flowcharts
- Identify decision points
- Specify variability of processing time and flow
- Insert controls/control points
- Assignment/identification of resources (e.g., people, technology)
- Specification of automation opportunities
- Documentation of process
- Test the process within real-world conditions
- Create methods/tools to monitor process performance

Notes:

   a. It is vital that process creation and process improvement or reengineering include full participation, or at least systematic input collection, from the people most familiar with existing service problems, customers, and problem recovery practices.

   b. Since service providers are not working from a blank sheet of paper and probably already have problem solving/recovery processes, proven tools for process improvement and reengineering should be employed (e.g., LEAN Six Sigma, gap analysis, root cause analysis).

2. Technology

Technology should be developed to, wherever possible, automate the problem recovery process. Such technology can be used to maximize all the elements of WACW (i.e., Accuracy, Timeliness, Access and so on).

- There is a myriad of methods (processes) to develop technology —both hardware and software. It is reasonable to state that all the methods have merit and none of the methods are perfect. It is beyond the scope of this discussion to make a qualitative selection of one approach versus another, except to assert that it is common wisdom that many technology development failures find their source in the early phases of the process, often during requirements gathering. Therefore, like process development, the technology development process should include full participation, or at least systematic input collection, from the people most familiar with existing service problems, customers, and problem recovery practices.

- The Software/System Development Life Cycle (SDLC) depicted on the right, used here only as an example, is a well understood and widely used set of steps in the application development process.

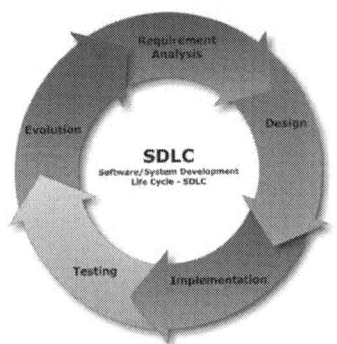

- It is also worth noting that, if the problem recovery process is fully automated or accomplished through customer self-service, the supporting technology (e.g., provider website, *must* be easy to access and use, with a way for the customer to sidestep the technology to reach a person (e.g., via a phone call, live chat).

3. People

People must be trained and experienced in implementing the problem recovery process and effectively using the enabling technology. Because everyone is a customer *and* a provider, the types of people engaged in problem recovery is almost limitless (we all make mistakes, and we all experience the result of someone else's mistakes). Defining a population as almost limitless makes it difficult to derive practical actions relative to that population. Thus, for the purposes of usefulness and clarity, what follows will focus on the classic model of a service provider engaged with an external customer.

In the classic model of service delivery, the provider might be interacting with their customer via a variety or combination of channels. These channels might include face-to-face communication, telephone communication (either one-on-one or via a call center), conference calls and video conferencing, or email and other computer mediated communication (e.g., text, chat).

An Interesting Anecdote: One of my customers had a reputation for "banding together" in the event of a problem. Teaming up within and between departments to deal with problems was a common occurrence. Initially, customers were impressed by and liked the team approach (i.e., *espirit de corps*). However, customers became a bit cynical about the provider when there was a pattern of patching problems, but not addressing the root cause and creating prevention strategies, which meant that problems tended to reoccur. It became a cliché within my customer's organization that service problems brought people together for a team effort. My customer was proud of this cultural attribute. But at the same time, my customer's customers grew weary of what they viewed as a bias toward firefighting versus fire prevention.

Chapter 6 on Responsiveness goes into detail about effective communication between providers and their customers via all the channels above, so that content will not be repeated here. However, as stated earlier, during problem recovery the stakes go up and the customer may be more likely to experience and express strong emotions. *How providers behave during problem recovery defines them and their organization*. Thus, communication behavior demonstrated by the provider during problem recovery is worth special focus.

To be an effective agent for problem recovery, provider personnel must be trained and given the opportunity to practice skills in each area of WACW from the perspective of problem recovery:

- **Accurate Recovery:** Provider personnel must be trained and capable of implementing the recovery process and using enabling technology to correct mistakes/errors. It is especially important that they be able to prevent problem reoccurrence or ongoing repetition. This is so important that it is reflected by a cultural meme, "Don't make the same mistake twice."

- **Timely Recovery:** Provider personnel must be able to use the process and technology to implement and ensure recovery according to the established standard (i.e., established as part of the process and technology testing phase). They must also be able to provide customers with the estimated (i.e., Timely Enough) or precise time (i.e., Precision Timeliness) it will take to recover, remembering that the customer's experience of time during recovery may feel longer than actual clock time.

- **Accessible Recovery:** Some customers, especially B2B customers, may want in-process access to the recovery process as well as end-process access. Especially with high magnitude service problems (e.g., involving high dollar amounts, critical medical test results), provider personnel may need to be directly accessible to the customer (e.g., providing direct line, extension number). Being inaccessible during problem recovery may, for some customers and some problems, represent an entirely new problem.

- **Useful Recovery:** Customer goals for using the results of the service process vary widely and depend on the service(s) sought. Some customers want information they will use for decision making. Others want guidance or directions they can use to accomplish their goal. Still others want precise data they'll use to remain current on an evolving situation. It's the same during problem recovery. It's up to provider personnel to develop an understanding of how the customer will use the outcome(s) of recovery. This may be self-evident based on the type of service problem or uncovered via question asking.

- **Responsive Recovery:** The behavior of service provider personnel always matters, but its impact, positive or negative, is magnified during problem recovery. The behaviors detailed in Chapter 6 on Responsiveness must be systematically trained and practiced by customer-facing service personnel. While some of these communication skills may already present in the behavioral repertoire of some service personnel, other skills are less likely to be present, much less at a level of mastery. Specifically, the reflecting skill, defined earlier as *empathy in action*, is rare among people in general, and thus, rare among client facing service personnel. While some might argue that communication skills—including the empathic reflection—are naturally evolved skills and people either have the skills or they don't, the point made here and elsewhere is that such skills can be taught and, with sufficient practice, mastered (supported by 40+ years of experience and the research of Carkhuff, Rogers, et.al.).

> **Responsiveness During Problem Recovery:** It can be considered axiomatic that it is better for the service to tell the customer about a problem, rather than have the customer discover the problem on their own.

A Special Note about Empathic Reflecting: As described in Chapter 6, the empathic reflection can take several forms (e.g., verbatim, interchangeable, a reflection of feeling). Perhaps surprisingly, the recommendation here is that reflecting the customer's feeling should be used with great caution or may even be absent during most service problem recovery circumstances. This position is taken for three reasons:

1. The customer may be experiencing and expressing a strong emotion. (See the next Chapter for more on handling the emotional customer.) Reflecting an emotion correctly can be very powerful, but it requires mastery of the skill at the highest level, anchored to long experience. If the reflection of feeling is wrong as perceived by the customer, it becomes another problem and may significantly increase customer dissatisfaction. Instead, service providers should focus their reflecting skill on the content or goal(s) expressed by the customer (e.g., the summary or interchangeable reflection). This communicates

understanding without the risk of an inappropriate or incorrect reflection of feeling.

2. Reflecting the feeling(s) expressed by another person is often associated with the therapeutic process, and customer service personnel are *emphatically* not conducting a therapy session. Reflecting feeling can quickly lead to an increasingly personal dialogue versus a business discussion.

3. Very much related to the preceding point, reflecting another person's feeling as well as the root cause for that feeling may open the classic "Pandora's Box." The customer may be unused to another person actively listening and communicating a high level of interest in what they are saying and feeling. Thus, they may "open up" to a person who demonstrates a high level of understanding. In turn, the customer may disclose feeling and content completely inappropriate to the business discussion. More importantly, the customer service person is not a therapist and will likely be unable to competently close the "box," once it is opened.

An important caveat to the three preceding points: As mentioned in Chapter 6 and elsewhere, some provider customer relations may evolve, over months and years, into personal relationships. Among these relationships may be a doctor with their patient, the CRM with their B2B customer, the certified financial planner with their customer, the long-term insurance agent, and the list goes on. In these cases, reflecting feeling, while still used with caution, may be viable in the broader context of the provider/customer relationship.

A Call to Action

Each of the preceding chapters ended with an example of how the WACW element could be applied in a real-world situation. This chapter is no different. This section will begin with a simple example of using a matrix that relates organizational elements to each component of WACW.

The reason the matrix is important reflects the basic axiom that a problem cannot be addressed until it is identified and categorized in a useful way.

> **Personal Note:** The following depicts an actual service problem I experienced while writing this chapter. Thinking back on other problems and talking with others about their experience with service problems, I was able to "plug" in all of these service problems and recovery strategies into the matrix.

Customer Service Problem and
Problem Recovery: Diagnostic Table

The Problem:

Purchased a blood pressure monitoring device online. Unable to set up the companion software on smartphone because of a (customer) mistake while creating a password. Requested a password reset to be sent via email. Never received the email. Spent a good hour with no positive result.

WACW	ORGANIZATIONAL ELEMENTS		
	People	Process	Technology
Accuracy		Instructions did not address problem (No FAQs)	Never received promised email for password reset.
Timeliness			
Access			Website and device too complex, offering too many options for typical customer. No "Quick Start." No way to go back to "Factory Settings."
Usefulness		Could not use device or linked software.	
Responsiveness			Was unable to access the input screen needed for a password reset.

Problem Recovery:

Called the 800 number for service. CSR walked through three different approaches to the problem. After 45+ minutes, problem solved.

WACW	ORGANIZATIONAL ELEMENTS		
	People	Process	Technology
Accuracy	CSR demonstrated complete, in-depth, accurate knowledge of both process and technology.		
Timeliness	Total time to resolve problem excessive (45+ minutes).		
Access	CSR answered call immediately after short list of menu prompts.		
Usefulness	Able to quickly use/apply guidance from the CSR.		
Responsiveness	CSR demonstrated polite, professional, and *very patient* behavior. CSR listened, demon-strated understand-ing of content.		

Result: Problem resolved. Customer satisfied, but not delighted. Prevention strategies might include fixing email request option, offer fewer options, provide customer with the process/technology tools and instruction for a complete *and easy* restart of installation process.

Notice: The problem was described under the organizational elements: Process and Technology. By contrast, problem recovery fell entirely under the "People" element and each component. This was because the customer (me) sought out a CSR. It can easily be imagined that someone experiencing the same problem could have used the provider website to resolve the problem and the elements of the recovery process would be Process and Technology along with the WACW components of Accuracy, Timeliness, Access, Usefulness, and even Responsiveness (if it was not already addressed under Access).

Use the matrices on the following pages to first describe a service problem and then use the second matrix to describe problem recovery—whether it was successful or not. Remember that for both the description and the resolution, you may only use a few cells on the matrix and, further, someone else experiencing the same problem my use different cells reflecting their and their provider's action and differing perspectives.

Customer Service Problem: Diagnostic Table

Problem Description: _____

_____

_____

WACW	ORGANIZATIONAL ELEMENTS		
	People	Process	Technology
Accuracy			
Timeliness			
Access			
Usefulness			
Responsiveness			

Problem Recovery Action Matrix

Problem Recovery (what "you" did): _____

_____

_____

WACW	ORGANIZATIONAL ELEMENTS		
	People	Process	Technology
Accuracy			
Timeliness			
Access			
Usefulness			
Responsiveness			

Now, on to the next chapter which focuses entirely on various ways to apply WACW.

Knowledge isn't power until it is applied.
—Dale Carnegie

Knowledge becomes wisdom only after it has been put to good use.
—Mark Twain

Logic is only the beginning of wisdom, not the end.
—Leonard Nimoy
(as Spock)

Chapter 8
Applications: Putting WACW to Work

Each of the preceding chapters ends with, "A Call to Action." This chapter is focused on some additional ways the components of WACW can be applied by service providers. Thus, this entire chapter is *a call to action*. The driving principle behind the content of this chapter has been restated toward the end of each of the preceding chapters. *It is only by applying WACW that it can be wholly understood and its full potential realized.*

The examples that follow may or may not be a perfect, or even good fit, for some service organizations. Organizational cultures, configurations, and available tools vary widely. Therefore, service providers are encouraged to shape and communicate WACW to fit their unique needs and application goals. In fact, some components of WACW may *not* be included in all the applications that follow. For example, using the components of WACW as a customer survey support tool, it may not be necessary, or even wise, to survey individual customers (versus B2B customers) about accuracy and timeliness since most provider organizations are (or certainly should) be tracking this information internally. It can be a mistake to survey customers about performance data the provider already has because the provider may have, at least for a time, achieved the best performance possible (e.g., 99.5%) and improving would be cost prohibitive. The principle here is don't ask the customer about performance metrics (or any attribute) that the provider is not able or willing to invest in changing.

The following WACW applications are described in this chapter:
1. WACW as a Customer Survey Tool
2. WACW as an Employee Performance Assessment Tool
3. WACW as a Training Tool
4. WACW as a New Employee Orientation Tool
5. WACW as Part of a Standard Agenda for B2B Meetings

1. WACW as a Customer Survey Tool

It is difficult to pinpoint when formal customer surveys began. It is fair to say that up until the early 1980s, service providers made themselves aware of customer sentiment via very simple annual

surveys or, even more likely, through talking with customers—often customers experiencing a service problem.

Fast forward to the third decade of the 21st century and there are literally thousands of books and scholarly articles on customer surveys, survey data collection, and using customer survey results. Not surprisingly, there are thousands of survey providers, from individual management consultants to organizations like Bain & Company and McKinsey (two of the three top U.S. consulting firms). Bain in particular has a niche in the customer survey field with Net Promoter. (Net Promoter, created by Fred Reichheld, a Bain Fellow, is a popular and widely used survey tool valued for its simplicity and usefulness of its results, although some critics claim that it is a flawed tool.)

This section is not presented as a substitute for developing a deep understanding about customer survey construction, methods of fielding a survey, maximizing response rates, and using survey results to improve service, retain customers, and even engender customer loyalty. This section is not a substitute for either developing in-house survey expertise or hiring experts with a proven track record. What this section does do is insert the components of WACW into the customer survey thinking process.

> The proposition here is simple: If the components of WACW are inclusive enough and correct in relation to the service provider's customer, it follows that some or all these components should be reflected in customer surveys.

Since individual customer surveys abound nowadays (arguably too many), it is important to keep them short (concise) and easy to complete. For example, many provider call centers ask customers to *"Stay on the line for a brief X question survey that will take under 5 minutes to complete."* These surveys can be effective, although it is likely that most customers who complete the survey are either very satisfied or very dissatisfied. (Most of the customers in the "middle" not having had an experience worth taking the time to complete even a brief survey.)

Individual Customer Surveys Incorporating WACW (Examples)

This survey might occur after a phone call to the provider contact center, via an email to the customer, on the provider's website, or even via a call back after a service encounter. The two short samples that follow are narrowly focused on surveying customers about telephone CSR behavior.

Also, the two samples that follow are event based. The first event is a customer calling the provider's contact center for service—assessing the customer' experience with Responsiveness. The second event is a follow-up survey to a customer service problem—assessing the customer's experience with Problem Recovery.

Assessing the customer's experience with Responsiveness (Example):

(*Customer*) Please rate your level of satisfaction with the responsiveness of the service representative you just spoke with.

- Your satisfaction with the extent to which the Customer Service Representative demonstrated their understanding of your service request or inquiry during the call.

- Your satisfaction with the extent to which the Customer Service Representative had the knowledge needed to respond to your inquiry or service request.

- Your satisfaction with the extent to which the Customer Service Representative presented information to you in a clear and easy-to-understand way.

The satisfaction scale below could be used for the foregoing questions:

1.0	2.0	3.0	4.0
Very Dissatisfied	Dissatisfied	Satisfied	Very Satisfied

- Now, a general question: How likely are you to recommend this provider to others?*

1.0	2.0	3.0	4.0
Very Unlikely	Unlikely	Likely	Very Likely

Note: On a paper/pencil or web-based survey, a space would typically be provided for customer "comments in support of the rating."

Assessing the customer's experience with Problem Recovery (Example):

(*Customer*) You recently experienced a service problem with (name of organization/company). Please rate your level of satisfaction with our problem recovery efforts on your behalf:

- Your satisfaction with the time it took to solve your service problem.
- Your satisfaction with the accuracy of our problem recovery results.
- Your satisfaction with your ability to access us (by phone, the web, or other means) to start or get an update on the problem recovery process.
- Your satisfaction with the outcome of the problem recovery.

The satisfaction scale below could be used for the foregoing questions:

1.0	2.0	3.0	4.0
Very Dissatisfied	Dissatisfied	Satisfied	Very Satisfied

---

* The "Recommend" question can be inserted in virtually all customer surveys. This kind of question is more "active" than asking for customer satisfaction. It's asking for customer intent.

- Now, a general question: How likely are you to recommend our company to others?[*]

1.0	**2.0**	**3.0**	**4.0**
Very Unlikely	Unlikely	Likely	Very Likely

> **A brief note about Response Scales:** Ordinal, or stack ranking scales, are useful in gaining the customer's hierarchical preference among several items or activities. An interval scale, used here, gathers responses using descriptors and data points with equal distance between adjacent points. Paper/pencil or web-based customer service surveys tend to use interval scales. Heated debate can often ensue, even among experts, when deciding on a rating scale (e.g., 1 to 5, 1 to 10, 1 to 7). Providers should be wary of such debate, since virtually all scales are simply a continuum and even experts can find it hard to precisely articulate the material difference between two adjacent points on the scale. Therefore, words are used to anchor the points on a scale. This is also why a four point, fully anchored scale, is provided here. A five-point, Likert type scale, is not used here because a 3 rating would typically be defined as Neutral or Neither Satisfied nor Dissatisfied. The position taken in Chapter 1 is echoed here, specifically—*People don't feel neutral.*

A B2B Survey Incorporating WACW (Example)

Provider surveys of B2B customers will tend to be longer and more detailed than those used with individual customers. If a provider is asking about Accuracy, for example, types of accuracy would be detailed (e.g., new account set up, accuracy of a specific report) along with using a rating scale and requesting commentary. Thus, each component of WACW would be described with a list of provider actions or attributes to be rated and commented on by the customer. This makes for a relatively long survey and may or may not be useful in improving service, since the provider may already be tracking its own performance using reliable methods and tools (as mentioned in

---

[*] The "Recommend" question can be inserted in virtually all customer surveys. This kind of question is more "active" than asking for customer satisfaction. It's asking for customer intent.

[181]

the beginning of this chapter). In this case, the customer may simply be presented with quantified performance results and asked about their satisfaction.

Reporting on provider quantified performance results and asking about customer satisfaction will work reasonably well when addressing the WACW components of Accuracy, Timeliness, and at least some aspects of Access (e.g., up time/down time) and Usefulness (e.g., regulatory reporting). However, when it comes to Responsiveness and Problem Recovery, more detail is warranted. For example, defining responsiveness, in part, as the ability of a provider representative (e.g., CRM) to, "listen and demonstrate understanding," and then asking for a customer rating and commentary. This process can also lead to a long survey, but useful results. However, providers should be aware when and if a B2B executive or manager delegates survey completion to personnel unfamiliar with the details and nuances of the B2B relationship—posing a threat to the validity of at least some survey results.

An effective alternative, albeit labor intensive and potentially costly, is to hire and deploy an expert in interviewing to speak to various B2B customer representatives—both at the executive and operational levels of the customer organization. This approach can be used in concert with more traditional survey approaches. The person interviewing B2B customers, after having done so, would document and present their findings. Findings can be organized to reflect the components of WACW. Once again, this approach is labor intensive and potentially quite costly. In addition, it requires the B2B customer to make various personnel available to be interviewed. This approach might be targeted at a limited number of strategic customers, but it is well worth it for the usefulness of the survey results. There's nothing that compares with the voice of the customer, *in their own words*.

A personal note about B2B Survey Interviews: For a little more than half of my 40-year career (so far), I've been involved in the development, implementation, and interpretation of both individual and B2B customer surveys. I typically hired or partnered with a credentialed and experienced survey expert, especially for constructing the statistical tools associated with the survey design, fielding, and interpretation of survey results. While my customers and I were generally satisfied with this survey work, the most successful and effective surveys I designed and implemented were one-on-one conversations with B2B customers.

For example, I conducted customer interviews for large financial service providers. I typically interviewed both senior executives (e.g., CEOs, CFOs) and operations executives (COOs, Operations VPs). The interviews usually lasted anywhere from a low of about 20 minutes to a high of 90+ minutes (some respondents had a lot to say, others didn't). The interviews were documented, always including exact quotes as well as my inferences about the underlying tone, beliefs, and feelings of interview respondents toward the service provider. In addition to documentation, I also gave interactive presentations about my findings to my customers. In turn, my customers were able to act based on the findings (e.g., identify opportunities, make specific process improvements, avoid future pitfalls).

The interview findings were generally presented in an order reflecting the evolution of the interview. But the results could also be organized to reflect all or most of the components of WACW—which was an affirmation of the WACW model I had been using for many years.

While I claim expertise in only a few areas, the most notable area is interpersonal communication. I have both undergraduate and graduate degrees in Psychology coupled with decades of practical experience in teaching and applying effective interpersonal communication skills. It is on that basis that I judge the B2B customer interview process and methods to be highly effective, at the same time recognizing that it could only be used with large B2B providers and customers and, even then, with a limited number of B2B customers. However, with the right training and process controls, provider personnel (e.g., CRMs) could come close to replicating the interview process described here with their B2B customers.

2. WACW as an Employee Performance Assessment Tool

Employee performance assessments, commonly referred to as employee performance appraisal, is often a bane in the existence of both employees and their managers. While many such systems exist, they often become a relatively meaningless, but time-consuming and a required task for managers as well as being a negative experience for many employees. The reality of the purpose of most appraisal systems is their use as a kind of check the box system for Human Resources departments and a tool for making performance-based compensation decisions. At worst, supervisors and managers are told ahead of time that a specific percentage of employees must fall into a certain category or receive a certain performance rating to align with corporate compensation goals. This kind of forced ranking or rating process is demoralizing at best and destructive at worst (e.g., punishing employees who are meeting the "standard" via the removal of a reward for doing so—to which the out-of-touch well paid executive often responds, *"Well, that's what they're paid for"*).

> **Personal Note:** The paragraph above is harsh and may earn the ire of many, especially HR professionals. In the interest of full disclosure, during the '90s I confess to creating what I thought was an effective performance appraisal system. My intent was good. I went to employees to build the content. I tested the system with the help of front-line supervisors. For a while (several months) the system seemed to work, at least for some people and some types of jobs. But over the long-term, the system was too complicated, hard to implement, time consuming, and became just another scheduled and painful event. "The road to Hell..." as they say.

The best of performance assessment or appraisal systems are continuous. They are not annual or bi-annual events. They are exemplified by a supervisor or manager being continuously aware of the performance of their staff—via both monitoring/observing and quantified performance reporting systems, and by these same supervisors and managers providing frequent and skilled feedback and other resources for performance management and, when necessary, performance improvement (e.g., training, coaching).

The components of WACW can be useful to structure a continuous performance assessment and for providing employee feedback. The following is formatted as a set of questions under each component of WACW. If a provider used this material, they would be wise to add and delete questions to shape the assessment to an individual employee or to team members sharing similar responsibilities.

Assessing Employee Accuracy

- How does each employee compare to other employees' performing the same tasks relative to accuracy and/or to accuracy standards (precision accuracy, accurate enough, telling the truth)?

- Are any employee errors the result of process flaws (which includes training) or are they a result of individual performance?

- Are employee errors isolated "one-offs," or do they represent a pattern in the employee's performance?

- What can be done if the employee is below the norm or shows a problematic pattern (e.g., make the employee aware, more frequent monitoring and feedback, further training, coaching, reassignment, or termination)?

- Does the employee demonstrate accuracy behaviors above in dealing with internal customers?

Assessing Employee Timeliness

All the assessment questions under accuracy apply to timeliness, so they won't be repeated here.

- In addition, is the employee productive relative to established expectations or standards?

- Does the employee manage the internal and external customer's experience of waiting time (see Chapter 3, for example, "Explained waits are experienced as shorter than unexplained waits")?

Assessing Employee Usefulness

- Is the work product of the employee perfectly useful, precisely conforming with customer requirements and supporting process/policy?

- If the situation warrants (e.g., setting customer expectations as a range of time) does the work product of the employee is useful enough (e.g., call-back between 4:30 to 5:00 p.m. EST)?

[185]

- Is the employee's communication with internal and external customers easy to use/understand (e.g., concise, well organized, good pace)?

Assessing Employee Responsiveness

- Is the employee unfailingly polite and professional with internal and external customers?

- Does the employee listen well, able to demonstrate understanding with internal and external customers (e.g., summary reflection, interchangeable reflection)?

- Does the employee ask effective—necessary and clarifying—questions and avoid leading/rhetorical questions?

- Does the employee communicate interest and attention in face-to-face interactions?

- Is the employee's verbal manner (e.g., tone, pace) sound professional and easy to follow?

- Is the employee's presentation of content complete and clear (i.e., similar to accessible)?

Assessing Employee's Ability to Recover from Problems

- Does the employee take accountability for mistakes or blame others or process/technology (without evidence)?

- Does the employee learn from mistakes and not repeat them?

- If the employee is in face-to-face or phone contact with the customer during problem recovery, does the employee apologize appropriately (without creating downstream liability), reflect the content of the customer's problem or experience, and make an appropriate commitment for problem recovery (e.g., timeframe)?

- If the problem involves a B2B customer or a strategically important customer, does the employee follow-up after recovery to ensure that the customer agrees that the problem has been resolved (thus, reminding the customer that the provider responded effectively to a problem)?

3. WACW as a Training Tool

Up until the end of WW II, training, when it was provided, tended to be technical (e.g., how to perform a specific function or use a piece of equipment.) The notable exception to this general statement comes from the military. Soldiers, going back to the Roman Empire and earlier, were trained in the "arts" of war. In fact, in the modern military, personnel are either engaged in an operation/mission or being trained and re-trained. Also in the military, personnel experience the benefits of repeated practice and feedback to continuously hone their skills, all part of the training model.

When it comes to training customer service employees, before the end of World War II, it was largely limited to learn by doing, shadowing a more experienced employee, or non-existent. By the 1960s and '70s, customer service training, while still minimal, benefited from the acceptance of the field of applied psychology, theorizing customer service skills could be taught, practiced, and monitored. From the '80s forward to the present-day, training in general and customer service training in particular has become ubiquitous.

Not surprisingly, along with the growth in customer service training came training fads promising simple answers to all possible challenges, no matter how complex. Examples of fads include Transactional analysis, neurolinguistic programing, TQM, Theory Z, and the list goes on. To be clear, each of the aforementioned fads have some value. They bring new knowledge, insight, and potentially positive results. But they are limited. It's not the fad that becomes destructive, instead it is the almost religious zeal of the fad's adherents. (While not discussed here, some of the current crop of personality tests qualify as fads. Again, not because the tests are entirely without merit, it's because some people form an emotional and often irrational bond with the fad.)

In the present day, it is reasonable to infer that almost all customer service providers train their employees. Even small providers deliver training, although it may be on the job training (OJT), systematic job shadowing (where the new employee "shadows" an experienced employee) or using publicly available in-person or online training. Large service providers often have dedicated training departments, employing full time experts in adult learning, curriculum design, and training delivery. (During COVID, much of this training has moved to online delivery, with mixed results.)

It is also reasonable to infer that existing service provider training includes training employees to work within the established process and to *access* and *use* provider technology to deliver *accurate* and *timely* customer service (italics used to highlight components of WACW). It may be a different story for behavioral skills training.

Behavioral skills, such as listening, presenting, and handling problems are often labeled as "soft skills." The position taken here is that this is a misnomer at best and, at worst, quite unhelpful. It reflects a pervasive but unstated belief among some providers that employees come to the job with "soft" skills, and that such skills can't be taught. They are intangible, ineffable. *Nothing could be further from the truth.* As stated in earlier chapters (especially 1 and 6) there is a vast body of peer reviewed research indicating that behavioral skills can be taught and, through practice and experience, mastered.[*]

Delivering behavioral skills training in a way that reflects WACW could include, but not be restricted to the following:

Behavioral skills related to *Access*: teaching employees to...

- Present content, especially technical information, in clear, easy to understand language.
- Present content using supportive (congruent) verbal mannerisms (e.g., tone, pace).
- Demonstrate interest and attention with body language (e.g., eye contact, no distracting behaviors) in face-to-face contact with customers.

Behavioral skills related to *Usefulness*: teaching employees to...

- Present guidance or instruction using clear, easy to understand language and supportive mannerisms and body language.

---

[*] See the research of George Gazda, Carl Rogers, Robert Carkhuff, Graham Bodie, et al.

- Use effective questions to test the extent to which the customer understands and will be able to use the information provided, with an expressed willingness to go back over content using different words if the customer doesn't understand (and may not be able to use) the guidance or instructions.

Behavioral skills related to *Responsiveness and Problem Recovery*: teaching employees to...

- Effectively greet the customer and set a positive tone for the service interaction.
- Use effective questions (e.g., direct, open ended) to gather input from the customer.
- Listen and accurately reflect customer input, goals, problem(s), etc.
- Reflect the feeling (emotion) clearly expressed by the customer (as appropriate).
- Provide information or guidance reflecting the customer's inquiry or service goal(s).
- Set clear expectations for follow-up or the problem recovery process.
- Leave an effective voice mail.
- Effectively use email or other communication channels (e.g., chat).

An additional note about training: Training, and especially behavioral skills training, may be the first thing cut when the provider is trying to reduce costs. Reducing costs is inevitable in the continuing life cycle of the provider's service organization. However, providers should consider the message sent to employees and even to customers when cutting training as one of its first steps in cutting costs.

4. WACW as a New Employee Orientation Tool

As new employees enter the provider's service organization, they experience a *teachable moment*. This is when the new employee is paying close attention. This means that what the employee is exposed to in the first minutes, hours, days, and weeks of their employment will leave a powerful impression. This is when the provider organization demonstrates its culture and values. All too often, one of the first things employees are exposed to are seemingly endless forms to complete, an often dry review of the employee handbook, or a benefits presentation (along with decision making by the employee). To be clear, these are important, even critical activities. They are often there to protect both the employee and the provider. They can't and shouldn't be dispensed with, but they may not be the *best* way to begin the relationship with the new employee.

An alternative to the beginning of the typical new employee orientation is to define the customer and to discuss what all customers want from their provider. This approach communicates what is important to the provider organization—its culture and its values.

> **Important Note:** What is probably expected at this point is the recommendation for using new employee orientation to define the customer and WACW. And that may be extremely effective. However, what is really recommended here is that the provider not waste the teachable moment; the provider should actively decide on the first and lasting impression it wants to make on its new employees —this is a strategically important decision.

If customers are defined as everyone, and the WACW is part of the new employee orientation, it is recommended here that it not be presented via lecture. Instead, in the hands of a skilled and seasoned facilitator, this content can be delivered interactively through dialogue between the facilitator and the new employees.

For example, the facilitator might begin by asking, *"What defines a customer? What attributes do customers possess and share?"* Almost no matter what the employees say in response, a skilled facilitator can begin building a definition that compares favorably with the following:

> *A customer is anyone in a position to feel satisfied or dissatisfied about what "you" do, and a customer is able to act on their satisfaction or dissatisfaction. This makes literally everyone a customer.*

The components of WACW can likewise be "built" to reflect the input of new employees. To be clear, if, for whatever reason the desired content does not emerge from discussion, it can be presented. But if the new employees can be guided to *discover* the content, it is more likely to be meaningful and remembered. Further, the facilitator may have to accept terminology different than that used here to describe WACW. For example, the employees may say that customers want their provider to "fix problems," or "fix mistakes" instead of ever using the phrase Problem Recovery. An effective facilitator can use alternative language by first reflecting understanding, and then building it into WACW and, at the same time, adding to the understanding of the employees.

> **Personal Note:** I've "built" the customer definition and the components of WACW hundreds of times with the input of groups of employees. It takes practice and an unwavering commitment to treating employee input with respect, but it can be done successfully. And even when the desired content doesn't emerge, it can be presented additively. An effective facilitator doesn't "trick" participants, they guide.

5. WACW as Part of a Standard Agenda for B2B Meetings

Compared to the preceding examples in this chapter, using WACW as part of a B2B meeting agenda is a simpler, more straightforward application. (It may also represent another avenue for surveying the B2B customer.) Before providing an example, it is important to acknowledge that the agenda for the meeting with the B2B customer would almost certainly contain agenda items other than WACW. The monthly, quarterly, or annual meetings with the B2B client might include:

- Strategic (long-term) and Tactical (short-term) goals of both the provider and the B2B customer.

- New developments and progress on projects.

- Discussion of expanding or reducing the relationship between provider and their B2B customer.

- Review of changes in the marketplace or the overall business environment (e.g., regulatory change).

- Special situations (e.g., an error involving a B2B board member, emergence of a special interest group among B2B customers).

Within the context of the larger agenda, mutual reporting and discussion of performance and goals relative to WACW might be quite fruitful, as well as providing a recurring set of touchpoints for subsequent meetings and the ongoing relationship.

Note: The review of accuracy findings for all WACW components would ideally include metrics of both provider and B2B performance, since both are dependent on the other in at least some areas. This means that planning for the meeting and presentations during the meeting would be a shared responsibility.

Also Note: As stated earlier, as each component of WACW is discussed, an informal and a mutual satisfaction question could be asked (e.g., *"How satisfied are you with performance in this area?"*). This might be accomplished by simply posing the question to the group, or perhaps more useful and appropriate, having response cards made up in advance to allow participants to respond confidentially, beyond identifying as provider or B2B customer.

Some examples of WACW as part of the Provider/B2B Customer meeting:

Accuracy

- Reporting on the (precision) accuracy/error rates for specific activities or transactions (e.g., new account setup, accuracy of fulfillments, accuracy of transaction processing for B2B customers).

- Accuracy of routine and *ad hoc* reporting; naming each along with an accuracy metric, if available/appropriate.

- Accuracy of estimates for completion of special or *ad hoc* projects (also found under Timeliness).

- Accuracy of information or data given to the provider by the B2B customer (e.g., volume estimates following an event, marketing campaign, new product launch).

- Reporting on efforts underway or planned to improve accuracy, if appropriate.

Timeliness

(Not surprisingly, the content below echoes content under Accuracy):

- Reporting on the (precision) timeliness rates for specific activities or transactions (e.g., new account setup, accuracy of fulfillments, timeliness of transaction processing for B2B customers).
- Timeliness of routine and *ad hoc* reporting; naming each along with a timeliness metric, if available/appropriate.
- Timeliness of estimates for completion of special or *ad hoc* projects (also found under Accuracy).
- Timeliness of information or data given to the provider by the B2B customer (e.g., volume estimates following an event, marketing campaign, new product launch).
- Reporting on efforts underway or planned to improve timeliness, if appropriate.

Access

- Reporting on the ease of access to the provider contact center (if relevant) as measured by, among other factors, sequence of menu prompts, ability to get to a live CSR (e.g., number of rings to answer), hold and transfer protocol and frequency.
- Contact center personnel (especially outsourced offshore), have the ability to interact with customers with clear, unaccented language. (Admittedly, this can be highly subjective and politically sensitive, but if customers find the verbal behavior of CSRs inaccessible, change needs to occur, e.g., additional training.)
- Reporting on the extent to which the provider call center provides "one stop shopping," equipping CSRs with the right skills, knowledge, authority, and technology to handle almost any customer request.
- Provider website accessed via computer or handheld device is easy to navigate, no more than two to three clicks away from successfully completing a transaction.

Usefulness

- Based on direct observation or surveys, reporting on information, data, or guidance provided by CSRs or the provider website is, when necessary, perfectly useful—matching with exactly what the customer wanted and their expectation for how they will use the delivered service.

- Similar to above, performance of the provider or the B2B customer on giving "useful enough" estimates or ranges when setting expectations with customers.

- The extent to which information, data, or guidance accessed from a contact center or technology channel is easy to use (as measured by actual customer use or input from users).

Responsiveness

- **Note:** If the provider call center (whether in-sourced or out-sourced) is using a behavioral checklist to monitor and report on performance (see Chapter 6), this would be presented and discussed here. If not, less formal monitoring and reporting might occur.

- Based on monitoring, the performance of the provider service personnel (e.g., CSRs, CRMs) in listening and demonstrating understanding when interacting with customers of all kinds (e.g., the customer, the customer's customer).

- Based on monitoring, the performance of the provider service personnel (e.g., CSRs, CRMs) in demonstrating effective verbal manner (e.g., tone, pace) and in face-to-face interactions, body language (e.g., eye contact, no distracting behavior).

- Based on the direct experience of B2B personnel, does the provider apply the skills of responsiveness in interactions with B2B personnel?

- Also potentially addressed here: Responsiveness of provider email, conference and video conferencing, chat, texting, etc.

Problem Recovery

- Overall review of service problems during a specific time period (e.g., since the last meeting). The type, frequency, and magnitude would be reviewed and assessed relative to standards (e.g., for accuracy, timeliness, (systems) access).

- Some problems might be selected for in depth review based on B2B customer preference, magnitude, repetition, the identity of the end-customer (e.g., strategically important, an internet influencer).

- Review of provider problem recovery processes and enabling technology. This would necessarily include a review of B2B process and technology, since at least some problems would be handled jointly.

- As possible, the provider and possibly B2B problem recovery behavior demonstrated by service personnel would also be reviewed (e.g., review of actual calls between the provider and customers, accuracy of expectation setting, communication to customers about problem recovery process and resolution).

Additional Notes about the Application of WACW

The foregoing application examples tend to focus on providers and their individual end customers or their service B2B customer. As stated many times in the preceding chapters, almost anyone can be defined as a customer, so some additional applications might include:

1. Using the components of WACW to assess the performance of supervisors, managers, and even senior executives in their role of provider to their employees as customers.

2. Using WACW to assess, and where necessary improve, the working relationship between two or more organizational work units or departments.

3. Some B2B service providers (both large and small) may outsource (subcontract) certain functions. The past two decades have seen dramatic growth in contact center outsourcing. The components of WACW, especially responsiveness (see Chapter 6), could be important, among other tools, in managing an outsource service provider, leading, for example, to Service Level Agreements.

[195]

4. Chapter 1 provides a discussion of internal and often overlooked customers (e.g., housekeeping, cafeteria, and security personnel). While all the components of WACW apply to these personnel, the behaviors of responsiveness when interacting with these personnel are especially relevant. This might be the subject of an important discussion during new employee orientation.

In summary, there is almost no provider customer relationship (e.g., internal, external, B2B) that would not benefit from being examined in relation to WACW. The epilogue that follows, "goes out on a limb," by selectively applying WACW to personal relationships.

...people will forget what you said, people will forget what you did, but people will never forget how you made them feel.

—Maya Angelou

I have never let my schooling interfere with my education.

—Mark Twain

Chapter 9
Applying WACW to Personal Relationships*

This epilogue represents a risk. The risk is that trying to apply WACW to personal relationships gives it one of the central features of a fad, the promise of almost infinite transferability. That is, the principles and components of the fad can be transferred from one setting to another without significant revision—in this case from a customer service setting to the relationships in your personal life. As fad moves to cult, as they often do, cult members will often insist that, not only is significant revision unnecessary when transferring the fad, it is forbidden—heretical.

As an offset to the fad risk, I encourage readers of this chapter to redefine the components of WACW to optimize its usefulness, to apply the underlying principles to personal relationships. For each WACW component that follows, I've offered alternative words and phrases to add to the flexibility of WACW applied to personal relationships. For me, WACW is like a microscope, giving the user a chance to observe underlying structures, but like a microscope, it is up the user to interpret and act on such observations.

Why try to apply WACW to personnel relationships? The answer is found in the definition of a customer used on all the foregoing chapters:

> *A customer is anyone in a position to feel satisfied or dissatisfied about what "you" do,* **and** *a customer is able to act on their satisfaction or dissatisfaction.*

---

* This chapter is written from a first-person perspective. It speaks directly to the reader. Previous chapters were explanatory and informational, anchored to my professional experience, insights, and the works and thoughts of other experts. This chapter represents my personal opinion and experience. My opinion is supported by the content in the previous chapters; this chapter is intentionally a very personal statement and application of the definition of a customer and WACW.

In previous chapters, the word "You" was literal (as it is in this Epilogue) and representational (representing the service provider organization). The point of this chapter is to assert that we all share the attributes of a customer, feeling situationally satisfied or dissatisfied with the people in our lives (e.g., friends, family members). And we all share the attributes of a provider, "serving" the people around us. And we, and they, can certainly all act based on feeling satisfied or dissatisfied.

The action that can be taken by a satisfied or dissatisfied customer, employee, colleague, etc. is described in earlier chapters (e.g., complain/compliment, decrease/increase business). The action that can be taken by a satisfied or dissatisfied person with whom I have a personal relationship will vary based on the situation and the relationship. For example, if I behave in a way that dissatisfies a friend (e.g., I'm rude, less than truthful), there may be no immediate action. However, if I behave poorly over a series of encounters, there *may* be an accumulation of dissatisfaction that leads to an erosion or even outright cessation of the relationship. I italicized the word "may" because effective problem recovery is always possible, and our personal relationships can often be salvaged after having been damaged. (Good friends may be quick to forgive if a genuine apology and behavior change is proffered.)

Family relationships are different. While we all know about families whose members have become estranged, the bonds of family are quite strong and problems may be at least tolerated and potentially resolved, even if it takes years. One family wild card is children. Every interaction I have with my children either affirms or expands my satisfaction. They can "push my buttons," make me angry, but at no point can I envision an end to the relationship. Brothers, sisters, spouses, and even some relations by marriage operate comparably, but not with the same potency as between a parent and child.

So, what do the people in our personal lives want?

Accuracy

Words or phrases that could be used in personal relationships that are equivalent to Accuracy include *honesty, genuineness, being forthright, correct, being truthful, trustworthy*, etc.

[198]

Precision Accuracy: At first glance, precision accuracy may not seem to apply to personal relationships. Giving it a second glance, however, I can certainly envision (and have experienced) the need for precision accuracy in personal relationships. It may seem a mundane example, but giving directions to others benefits from precision. If I'm telling someone how to get somewhere or how to do a technical task, being imprecise could leave the other person feeling dissatisfied. Remembering certain dates precisely may also apply to personal relationships (e.g., birthdays, anniversaries). By contrast, forgetting an important date can be problematic—so much so that a husband forgetting an anniversary is a kind of a cliché in our culture.

Accurate Enough: This applies readily to personal relationships. When offering an opinion, observation, perception, or directions to another person, most often such content doesn't need to be precise, but it should be accurate enough. I used the example of a cooking recipe and the phrase, "a pinch of salt" as an example of accurate enough. The content we present in our personal relationships and our listening behavior needs to be accurate enough to sustain a meaningful, productive, even fulfilling conversation.

Accuracy as Truth: People want the truth. They want us to tell the truth. They *don't* want us to lie. They want us to respond truthfully to questions and express our comments and opinions in discussion in a way that is, to the best of our knowledge, genuine or true. All of that being said, we don't say everything that comes into our head, especially when doing so would likely be perceived as insensitive, rude, or even hurtful. Benjamin Franklin said, *"Thinking aloud is a habit which is responsible for most of mankind's misery."* In fact, be wary of people who routinely say rude or hurtful things and defend this behavior by proudly claiming that they are "only saying what's true," or "I'm only saying it like it is." What they are saying may be empirically true, but their motivation is suspect. They may simply enjoy hurting the feelings of others, or they may think, quite wrongly, that they're being entertaining or colorful. They're being neither.

Timeliness

Words or phrases that could be used in personal relationships that are equivalent to Timeliness include *being available, being dependable* (relative to time), *punctual, being respectful* (relative to time).

Precision Timeliness: As with precision accuracy, precision timeliness may not seem applicable to personal relationships. After all, we don't typically have to agree to or promise precise expectations for timeliness in our personal relationships. On occasion though, we might. For example, if a friend or family member and I have a specific appointment at a specific time (e.g., doctor/specialist appointment), precision timeliness may come into play. For another example, if I'm meeting a friend on a video call (e.g., Zoom), I want to be available at precisely the time set. In this second example, I could be early in order to be available at that precise time.

Timely Enough: Being timely enough is easily applied to our personal relationships. Timely enough means being within a stated, implied, or mutually understood range of time. *"I'll see you at about 8 o'clock,"* is timely enough for a social encounter. Even, *"I look forward to seeing you tomorrow,"* may be sufficient in the context of a personal relationship (or even in a business setting, under certain circumstances). Timeliness has a cultural variable. For example, being 5 or 10 minutes in most western cultures is within the range of acceptability. Timeliness may also reflect individual variables. For example, throughout my career I took pride in almost never being late. In fact, I was often early. In a social setting, being early may pose its own problems (e.g., being early to social gathering is not a good idea). Be wary of people who are perennially late, often very late, making others wait, leading to high levels of irritation and dissatisfaction. Always being late is rude and disrespectful. It may be that the person who is always late is trying (and failing) to exercise power in the relationship.

Timely as Fast or Faster: A friend or family member reaches out and asks for immediate help. They want a fast response, faster than the norm in the relationship. They may want us to share their sense of urgency. Remember in Chapter 3, concerning timeliness, that a person's perception of time can be quite subjective. Thus, in a tense, stressful, or otherwise difficult situation a person may experience a wait of 1 minute as 5 minutes, a wait of 5 as 10 or 15 minutes, and so on. What can you do to help? Certainly, first and foremost, if you can address the urgent need, do so (e.g., provide the help they need as fast as possible). Also, remember the research of David Maister (again, see Chapter 3). For example, "occupied time feels shorter than unoccupied time." Occupy your friend or family member's time with listening and demonstrating your understanding (more thoroughly addressed later under Responsiveness). Be wary of those who express urgency as a default response to almost any situation. Not every problem or need requires a fast or faster response. In fact, for some problems or needs, a fast or faster response may be exactly the wrong thing to do (e.g., going into a panic over a missed appointment does not necessarily require a speedy resolution). In fact, you may want to slow things down by talking the panicked person down from the feeling, again by listening and showing understanding. (**Note:** In no instance should you tell the person to "calm down" or "don't panic." These phrases will likely increase the person's expressed feelings, as well as being quite irritating.)

Access

Words or phrases that could be used in personal relationships that are equivalent to Access include being approachable, self-disclosure, forthcoming, available, open, accessible, welcoming, understandable, etc.

You will recall in Chapter 4 that access was described relative to face-to-face, telephone, and internet-based contact. Personal access echoes these channels of communication. Family and friends can interact with me face-to-face, over the phone, and via technology (e.g., FaceTime). But in our personal relationships, access takes on special meaning. Being accessible to friends and family goes beyond simply being physically available. It also means being emotionally present and being open to the narrative and feelings expressed by family and friends. It may also include a willingness to engage in self-disclosure, describing experiences and reactions relevant to or comparable to the narrative and feeling presented by others. (Remember that saying something like, "I know what you mean," is not effective self-disclosure.)

Being accessible overlaps with useful in that the language you use needs to be understandable (accessible) to the person you are speaking with. Using inappropriate terminology (jargon), talking down to someone, or being patronizing can also make you inaccessible, or, as the English put it, "off-putting." Added to this, being crude or expressing inappropriate bias (e.g., gender bias) can also be very off-putting. In one sense, the often-used phrase, "know your audience," comes to mind. Since I'm addressing personal relationships, it might be assumed

[201]

that you already know your audience. However, especially early in a personal relationship, you need to make a concerted effort to learn the likes and dislikes of the other person and, even more specifically, their values. It's a mistake to assume you share values with another person unless you have sufficient experience to do so. For example, I have a customer/provider relationship with someone who I also think of as a friend. We've known each other for many years. We share many values (e.g., for honesty, integrity), but not all. To ensure continued mutual access, we've both tacitly agreed to avoid certain topics. Rather than limiting our friendship, the decision not to talk about certain things has strengthened our relationship. We respect each other's differences. Obviously, in other relationships, significant and broad differences in values might preclude the evolution of a friendship.

Be wary of being, "the strong silent type." While this attribute is often cast as positive and attractive, it can make a person who evinces this trait inaccessible—closed off. Be equally wary of being, or people who "wear their heart on their sleeve," to an excessive degree. Most of us want the people with whom we have a personal relationship to be willing to disclose their feelings and underlying reasons. At the same time, it can be uncomfortable and even tedious to be with someone whose feelings are *always* on full display.

Usefulness

Words or phrases that could be used in personal relationships that are equivalent to Usefulness include *utility, valued opinion/advice, understandable, applicable, benefit, value, worthwhile,* etc.

When we hear the word useful, we automatically see the word *use*, as in using other people. This seems somehow antithetical to a personal relationship, let alone friendship. It isn't. One thing, among many, that I appreciate about the friends I have is that they are willing to listen to me and then offer useful opinions, advice, or ask clarifying questions. And they remain friends even when I don't agree with or act on their input. *Frequently, what is most useful is simply having someone who is willing to listen.*

I have a good friend of many years who is one the most capable people I've ever known. He can rebuild cars, rehabilitate old houses, do plumbing, electrical work, and the list goes on. He's also an avid reader of non-fiction, plays the piano, and is an accomplished power lifter. If I have a problem or project in any of his areas of expertise, I'm likely to call him and invariably get useful input. However, we're not friends because of all his abilities. We're friends because we share many of the same values and our mutual willingness to help one another. Also, what compliment can one person give to another that is greater than asking for their advice or opinion?

Another example of usefulness applied to personal relationships happens within families, specifically between parents and their children. It is absolutely within a parent's job description to provide useful information to their children. Perhaps more important is the usefulness of the parent modeling positive behavior and values that can then be adopted (*used*) by their child.

Be wary of people who offer opinions, advice, or direction on every topic under the sun, even in areas for which they have no experience, much less useful knowledge. Some people feel obliged, or that they have the right, to weigh in on any and all topics. Their input may not only be useless, but it may also be flat-out wrong, even dangerous (e.g., someone offering health advice with no valid knowledge base or credentials).

Responsiveness

Words or phrases that could be used in personal relationships that are equivalent to Responsiveness include *empathy, listening, positive body language and verbal manner, understanding, presenting,* etc.

Similar to the opening of Chapter 6 covering service provider responsiveness, I'll begin this brief section with verbal behaviors that are, woefully frequent in our personal lives, but almost completely unresponsive. For example, *"I understand what you mean," "I know how you feel,"* and, even worse, *"You shouldn't feel that way."* Go back to Chapter 6 for more examples but suffice to say the unsupported claim of understanding or the denial of another person's perspective are, as well as being rude, non-responsive, ineffective, and in some cases, damaging to a relationship.

The above being said, unresponsive behaviors may be present in our personal relationships. Forgivable, if the behaviors are infrequent, but problematic if they represent a pattern of behavior. It may be reflected in the difference between acquaintances and people with whom we are friendly versus those people we consider to be good, even life-long friends.

Responsiveness is the willingness to listen and to demonstrate interest and, when possible, understanding. It is the ability and willingness to do the work necessary to understand another person's perspective or feelings and to reflect that understanding via a genuine verbal reflection. Responsiveness also means communicating interest and attention via body language (e.g., eye contact, nodding) and via verbal manner (e.g., tone, the use of silence). Asking effective, non-leading questions and presenting your perspective in a way that is helpful (useful) to another person is also part of being responsive. Once again, Chapter 6 can be revisited for a more thorough description of the details of responsiveness. While Chapter 6 is focused on the service provider/customer relationship, all the behaviors described in the chapter can readily be applied to your personal relationships.

Be wary of people who aggressively reflect. An anecdote will illustrate this problem. A friend and colleague of mine related an experience he had with a person I had trained in the skills of responsiveness—specifically the reflecting skill. Apparently, the person I trained took the content to heart and *always* tried to reflect what she was hearing and did so aggressively. My friend and colleague said he felt "assaulted" by her constant reflections and the tone she used. This is an example of a positive and useful skill—reflecting—becoming negative because of over and inappropriate use, coupled with an aggressive tone of voice. Remember, the key to the reflecting skill (and every other skill) is to be able to use it and then choose the right time and application. I'm reminded of a quote from Abraham Maslow, *"If the only tool you have is a hammer, it's tempting to treat everything as if it were a nail."* Reflecting is not the only tool in your interpersonal skills arsenal.

Problem Recovery

Words or phrases that could be used in personal relationships that are equivalent to Problem Recovery include *problem solving, resilience, salvage, handling mistakes, overcoming a setback, meaningful apology,* etc.

We all make mistakes in our working lives. We all make mistakes in our personal lives. As I've said in Chapter 7 and elsewhere, it's not our mistakes that define us, we're defined by what happens next—by how we respond to our mistakes. How we respond expresses our values and core personality as well or better than any other trait we demonstrate.

All the mistakes we make in our personal lives can be logically organized under the preceding components of WACW. The following provides an example:

WACW Component	Example of Problems in Our Personal Relationships
Accuracy	I tell a lie or present the truth in an unnecessarily hurtful manner.
Timeliness	I'm *avoidably* late for an event that is of high importance to another person.
Access	I withhold my perspective or feeling when engaging in self-disclosure would have been helpful.
Useful	The information I provide is incomplete or irrelevant to the specifics of the situation.
Responsiveness	I claim understanding without proof or deny the feeling expressed by another person.
Problem Recovery	I make the same mistake repeatedly.

A generic template for recovering from problems in our personal lives would include:

- A genuine apology, *"I'm sorry..."*. **Not** a qualified apology, *"I'm sorry, but I tried my best,"* or *"I'm sorry,* **but** *I didn't have the information I needed."* Leave out the word *"but."*

- Take accountability, *"This is on me, no excuse."* (Don't blame someone else or the situation. Own it.)

[205]

- Reflect what happened, *"You're disappointed because I didn't listen."* (Be careful. You can reflect feeling and content or only content. If you have doubts about feelings, stick with content.) **Note:** This may come first depending on the situation. It clarifies your apology.

- Make a commitment, *"Moving forward, I'll...".* (This can be as general or as specific as the situation warrants, e.g., *"I'll be a better listener,"* *"When you talk about X, I'll withhold my perspective (shut up) until you are finished."*)

Be aware that, if you make the mistake repeatedly, any apology you offer will feel less and less genuine to the other person. You'll need to apologize for the repetition as an additional mistake you made. Then you need to get to work on *not* repeating the same mistake again (and again).

Thankfully, our close friends and family may be willing and even eager to forgive a mistake, as long as the mistake is acknowledged, and accountability is expressed. Likewise, you should be willing and eager to forgive a mistake. To paraphrase Shakespeare in the *Merchant of Venice*, "The quality of **forgiveness** is not strained."

Be wary of the person who routinely apologizes and continues to *willfully* demonstrate the objectionable behavior. I'm embarrassed to admit that I've been guilty of this. I have a relative by marriage about whom I've been almost unrelentingly sarcastic. Not surprisingly, my behavior was returned in kind. There is no mutual satisfaction in this relationship. (You'd think I'd know better.)

*****

In the final analysis, this section, and in fact this entire book, is about knowledge and skills; knowledge about the nature of all our customers, the parts of a service organization and what our customers want, and the skills needed to predictably deliver satisfaction to all our customers and to the people in our personal lives. The power of a skill is that, with sufficient effort, it can be learned, practiced, and mastered. And with mastery, the skills become a kind of art.

Become an artist.

About the Author

David Driskill has had his consulting and training firm for over 40 years. Mr. Driskill has served his clients as a consultant, educator, and researcher in a number of fields, including Financial Services, Health Care, and Law Enforcement. In Financial Services, he is a founding partner of National Quality Review, a well-respected service quality research and consulting firm. David is widely known as an effective teacher and presenter, as well as being a frequent speaker at industry conferences. As a consultant, he has a reputation for problem solving, managing strategic change, and project execution. He has authored a book, *You Are the Voice of Your Company,* (HRD Press 2006) and a variety of white papers and training curricula on topics ranging from, Tone, Words & Empathy for Telephone Customer Service, Making Effective Presentations, Effective Problem Recovery, and Conflict Management. For a series of YouTube videos created by David, see www.daviddriskill.com.

Mr. Driskill takes the position that rather than "soft skills," specific behavioral skills can be taught, practiced, and mastered. In turn, these skills are instrumental in effective communication, client service, conflict resolution, influence, problem recovery, and an array of other professional and personal applications.

Mr. Driskill attended the Chicago City College system, Governor's State University, American International College, and the University of Chicago. Mr. Driskill received a BA and an MA in Psychology.

Comments about the Book and the Author

"In this intellectually rigorous and practical guide, David Driskill has distilled a lifetime of listening to customers into timely and timeless principles for superior customer service. The breadth and scope are astonishing." – David R. Giardino, Design Thinking Coach

"David's book opened my eyes to the critical role we all play in satisfying all of our various customers (internal and external) and more importantly, the steps necessary to put your company in a path to success." – Michael Dean, Managing Director, Financial Services

"David has a unique passion and ability to help others focus on the voice of the customer. This book is a must read for any organization going through a transformation or simply wanting to improve their engagement model." – Andrew Wise, International Deputy Chief Transformation Officer, State Street Corporation

*"Open any page in this book and you'll find insights learned from decades of work as a quality guru in the service industry. Driskill takes the oft-stated concept **everyone is a customer** and shows how to integrate people, processes, and technologies to deliver consistently superior results—to all kinds of customers, all of the time."* – Max Stites, Director (ret.), Capital Group Companies

"As a consultant, David always figured out how to get the job done, often having to navigate the multiple agendas of a large and complex organization. As a trainer, David brought both classroom and real-world material to his courses, always demonstrating what may be his biggest asset, his listening skills. He is the consummate problem solver." – Steve Hooley, CEO at DST Systems

"Working with our national financial services firm, David effectively leveraged his deep industry knowledge and excellent skills as a listener. He quickly earned the respect and trust of our management and employees. His recommendations pinpointed process improvement areas. Then he led well received training sessions to implement changes." – Dale Siligmueller, CPA, Siligmueller & Norvid Wealth Advisors

Made in the USA
Middletown, DE
16 July 2023

34654760R00130